The Simpler The Better

Sensational Home Cooking

in 3 Easy Steps

Sensational Home Cooking in 3 Easy Steps

Sensational Italian Home Cooking in 3 Easy Steps

Sensational One-Dish Meals in 3 Easy Steps

THE SIMPLER THE BETTER

SENSATIONAL HOME COOKING IN 3 EASY STEPS

Leslie Revsin

WILEY

JOHN WILEY & SONS, INC.

For general information on our other products and services please contact our Customer Care Department within the United States at (800) 762-2974, outside the United States at (317) 572-3993 or fax (317) 572-4002.

Wiley also publishes its books in a variety of electronic formats. Some content that appears in print may not be available in electronic books. For more information about Wiley products, visit our web site at www.wiley.com.

Library of Congress Cataloging-in-Publication Data:
Revsin, Leslie.
The simpler the better : sensational home cooking in 3 easy steps / Leslie Revsin.
     p. cm.
Includes index.
ISBN 0-471-48231-5 (Cloth)
1. Quick and easy cookery. I. Title.
   TX833.5.R48 2005
   641.5'55--dc22   2003019430

Book design by Richard Oriolo
Front cover photography: Duane Winfield
Insert and back cover photography: David Lazarus
Prop stylist: Stephanie Basralian

Printed in the United States of America

10 9 8 7 6 5 4 3 2 1

For

Max and Henry,

my best boys

Contents

Tender Meats

From American favorites like Salt and Pepper Burgers and BBQ Pork to dishes with more international flair like Pork Chops with Jalapeño Tomato Sauce, these recipes take the lead in offering easy dinners.

Vegetable Side Dishes

Vegetables served simply highlight fresh produce and make an appealing accompaniment to any meal. Tender Lemon-Caper Carrots and crisp Stir-Fried Broccoli with Garlic are flavorful sides, or try Grilled Zucchini with Balsamic Dressing for an outdoor touch.

Comforting Carbs

Definite crowd pleasers like Silver Dollar Corn Cakes, Savory Cheddar Cheese Muffins, and Smashed Potatoes with Fresh Basil are sure to go fast at the table.

Salads of All Sorts

Whether you need an elegant side dish, a simple starter, or a crisp lunch, salads always satisfy. Grilled Shrimp Salad with Feta Cheese and Olives and Smoked Chicken and Mango Salad stand beautifully on their own. Or add an appealing side dish of Baby Spinach Salad with Warm Bacon Dressing or sassy Lemon Coleslaw.

Simple Sweets

A sweet treat is the best ending to a lovely supper. Pecan Candy is great alone, or add the crisp, sweet nuts to a Chocolate Mocha Sundae. Dressed-up fruit is great for dessert, too: Blueberries with Maple-Orange Yogurt Sauce or Raspberries with Butterscotch Cream.

Acknowledgments

Writing a book can be a solitary affair, particularly when you're neck deep in it. But my friends and family were with me throughout this whole process. In fact, even when the book was little more than a fuzzy notion, their enthusiasm was contagious. And once the work actually began, they eagerly offered suggestions and gave me feedback that quickly became invaluable.

These are the special people I'd like to thank:

Sue Davis and Kate Johnson for cheering on the concept from day one.

Marie Zazzi, Cecile Lamalle, Liz Kaplan, and my daughter, Rachel Ramstad, for tossing great ideas and recipe possibilities my way.

My husband, Philip Carlson, for putting up with all the dinners made from dishes that didn't go together. Then the endless discussions about each one. His comments hit the mark much more than they missed.

Stephanie Basralian, my prop sylist, for understanding exactly what was needed.

My photographer, David Lazarus, for his great good will and great good style.

And last but certainly not least, my two Susans. Susan Ginsburg for her warm, smart, wonderful self, and for taking unsurpassed care of me as an agent. And my editor Susan Wyler, for her brilliant vision and piercing intelligence, and for our friendship.

Introduction

This book all came about because of my daughter, Rachel. When her son Max was born, she juggled the double job of being a mom with her freelance work and still managed to find time for cooking. Then little Henry arrived, and Rach soon found that all her time was disappearing at a rapid rate which dismayed her because she loves spending time in the kitchen. Hmm, I thought . . . how to help when they're out on the West Coast and I'm here in the East?

It didn't take long to imagine the sort of cookbook she needed. It was the kind anyone with limited time but lots of desire to cook would want. I kept thinking, and I came up with this: "Pared-down cooking. Really good food. And no gimmicks." I was excited. *The Simpler The Better* was born!

Let me tell you more about it. When you flip through the recipes in this book, you'll see they are short and to the point. Each has just the number of ingredients it needs to taste good, no more and no less. You'll see, too, that sometimes an ingredient does double duty. Take the Grilled Chicken Kebabs in Rosemary Yogurt, for instance. The rosemary yogurt is used twice: first as a marinade for the chicken in its raw state, then as a sauce for the cooked kebabs. The end result means fewer items to buy and quicker preparation time, too.

There's no need to search the globe to make this food. All the ingredients are from the supermarket and discount club. As for cooking times, they're thirty minutes and under, with many a good deal under. The cooking also calls for as few pots and pans as possible. After all, why use two pots when one will get the job done?

On top of that, some of the recipes include a technique or two that may surprise you (which makes the doing more fun, I think). Chunky Potato Soup in a Skillet is one of those with its topsy-turvy cooking method. Here's what I mean: The potatoes are cooked with onions, olive oil, and water in an open skillet until the water is all gone. Then the onions start to brown, which adds more flavor to the broth. "What broth," you say? The broth you've just added to turn it into a soup.

Navigating the book is simple. The recipes are easy to find, since the chapters are divided into everyday courses of soup, pasta, mains, side dishes, salads, and desserts. The book also has tips and pointers for making the recipes. Basically, I offer three different kinds of information:

The *Variations* you'll see in many recipes offer suggestions for ingredient substitutions, simple ways of varying a dish, or alternative cooking methods.

Each *Simple Tip* explains how to choose an ingredient, the kind of cookware to use, or the key technique in making the dish.

Dress It Up is for when you want to take a small extra step and add a flourish to the dish. Maybe because company's coming, or simply because you're in the mood.

This book was written with love. I hope you'll love it, too.

The Simpler The Better

Sensational Home Cooking

in 3 Easy Steps

Quick Homemade Soups

Creamy Avocado Soup

Light as a cloud and full of lush avocado flavor, this soup has big pieces of tender, browned onion and bits of jalapeño drifting through it. A perfectly ripe California avocado, one of the bumpy-skinned ones, is the best kind to use.

1 medium onion
1 large jalapeño pepper
1 tablespoon olive oil
2 ¾ cups chicken broth
1 ripe avocado

1 Coarsely chop onion. Seed and finely chop jalapeño.

2 Heat olive oil in a large saucepan over medium heat. Add onion and cook, stirring, until edges are well browned, 3 to 4 minutes. Add jalapeño and cook, stirring, 1 minute. Add broth, reduce heat to low, and simmer soup base until onion is tender, about 5 minutes.

3 Cut avocado in half and discard pit. Using a large spoon, scoop out avocado, making sure you get all the dark green bits near the skin. Puree avocado with 1 cup soup base in a blender until avocado is smooth, 15 to 30 seconds. Leave

bits of onion and jalapeño; they add color and texture. Stir avocado puree into remaining soup base in saucepan and reheat over low heat. Season with salt and pepper to taste. Serve hot.

4 SERVINGS

SIMPLE TIP *To pit and peel an avocado, first cut it in half lengthwise and twist open to separate the halves. Give the pit a light whack with a large knife so the blade sticks in part way. Then pull out the pit. Cut the avocado halves in half again and peel off the skin.*

DRESS IT UP *Garnish each serving with a scattering of fresh cilantro leaves or chopped dill.*

Black Bean and Bacon Soup

In addition to the bacon, onion, and jalapeño pepper, this black bean soup is seasoned in two ways. First, half is sautéed in rendered bacon fat and simmered along with the beans to deepen the flavor. The other half doesn't get cooked at all. Instead, it's stirred into the soup right before serving to add a salsalike finish.

6 strips bacon
3 large garlic cloves, minced
1 large jalapeño pepper, seeded and finely chopped
1 medium onion, finely chopped
2 cans (15 1/2 ounces each) black beans, liquid reserved
1 can (14 1/2 ounces) vegetable broth

1   Cook bacon in a large saucepan over low heat until crisp, about 5 minutes. Drain on paper towels. Leave fat in the pan.

2   Stir garlic and half each of jalapeño and onion into bacon fat. Cook 2 minutes, stirring. Add beans and their liquid, broth, and salt to taste. Simmer 10 minutes.

3 Puree ¾ cup of soup in a blender until smooth. Stir into remaining soup. Add remaining jalapeño and onion, and season with pepper to taste. Serve hot, with crumbled bacon on top.

4 TO 6 SERVINGS

SIMPLE TIP *Foam forms on the top of this soup as it simmers. To remove it, tilt the pot so the froth gathers on one side. Then you can skim it off easily with a large kitchen spoon.*

DRESS IT UP *Garnish each bowlful with a dollop of sour cream and thinly sliced scallion.*

Thai Chicken Noodle Soup

Get out the chopsticks! This soup is loaded with long, slippery noodles that slide right off the spoon. It's also seductively sweet and rich with coconut milk, fresh ginger, subtle spices, and tender chicken.

4 ounces skinless, boneless chicken breast

3 $\frac{1}{2}$ ounces flat rice sticks (half of a 7-ounce box)

1 can (13 $\frac{1}{2}$ ounces) coconut milk

1 $\frac{1}{4}$ cups chicken broth

$\frac{3}{4}$ teaspoon grated fresh ginger

$\frac{3}{4}$ teaspoon ground cumin

$\frac{1}{4}$ teaspoon ground cinnamon

1 tablespoon fresh lime juice

1   Cut chicken into small dice. Bring a large pot of water to a boil over high heat, then remove from heat. Submerge rice sticks in hot water. Soak 3 to 5 minutes, until tender-chewy; drain.

2   Heat coconut milk and chicken broth in a large saucepan over medium-low heat. Whisk in ginger, cumin, and cinnamon. Season with lots of pepper. When hot, add chicken and cook 1 minute. Stir in lime juice.

3   Divide noodles among 4 bowls. Ladle soup over noodles and serve hot.

4   SERVINGS

SIMPLE TIP *If the noodles stick together before you're ready to serve them, run them quickly under warm running water. Then give the colander a good shake and divide them among the bowls.*

DRESS IT UP *Scatter crunchy bean sprouts over the top of each serving and garnish with fresh leaves of cilantro or fresh mint.*

Chilled Greek Eggplant Soup

Thanks to its refreshing yogurt base, this silken soup is perfect for a steamy summer night. When you first make it, you may say, "Where's the soup?" because it's so thick with eggplant. Taste a spoonful, though, and the balance will reveal itself.

$3/4$ pound eggplant

2 tablespoons olive oil

$1/2$ cup chopped roasted red bell peppers

1 large garlic clove, minced

$3/4$ cup plain yogurt

$1/2$ teaspoon dried oregano

1   Slice ends off eggplant, then peel. Chop into small pieces.

2   Heat olive oil in a large saucepan over low heat. Stir in eggplant. Cover and cook 2 minutes, then add $1/4$ cup water. Cook, covered, stirring occasionally, until eggplant is very tender and water is gone, 6 to 8 minutes. Add roasted peppers and garlic. Cook, uncovered, stirring, 2 minutes. Remove from heat.

3 Stir in 1^1/$_2$ cups cold water and then yogurt. Season with oregano and salt and pepper to taste. Chill until cold. Stir before serving.

4 SERVINGS

SIMPLE TIP *For a quick chill, set the soup in a bowl of ice water and stir it occasionally.*

DRESS IT UP *Sprinkle each serving with slivered fresh mint leaves.*

Green Gazpacho

Fresh spinach, cucumber, and bell pepper make up the bright palette in this pretty green soup. All that's required is a little chopping, then a quick whirl in the blender.

2 large Kirby cucumbers
1 small green bell pepper
1 bag (10 or 12 ounces) spinach, preferably prewashed
2 large garlic cloves, chopped
$1/4$ cup plus 2 tablespoons extra-virgin olive oil

1   Peel and slice cucumbers. Cut bell pepper in half and discard seeds and ribs; coarsely chop. Remove any coarse stems from spinach.

2   In 2 batches, puree garlic, cucumbers, and bell pepper with olive oil in a blender or food processor until smooth, about 2 minutes. Taste and, if necessary, thin slightly with up to $1/2$ cup cold water. Season with salt and pepper.

3   Chill until cold. Stir before serving.

4 SERVINGS

SIMPLE TIP *Substitute about two-thirds of a regular cucumber for the Kirbys, but be sure to scoop out its seeds before pureeing. And you may not need to chill the soup if it's made with vegetables straight from the refrigerator.*

DRESS IT UP *For an elegant finish, float a thin slice of lemon over each serving. For a rustic touch, toast a slice or two of French or Italian bread and brush with olive oil. Tear the bread into small croutons over each serving.*

VARIATION *Serve each bowl with a lemon wedge on the side for squeezing into the gazpacho.*

Chilled Melon Soup with Fresh Basil

This refreshing froth of a soup is the essence of summer melon enhanced with a sparkle of lime and a smattering of basil. Honeydew makes a lovely pastel green version, and cantaloupe, one the color of coral.

1 (3-pound) honeydew or other melon
$1\frac{1}{2}$ tablespoons fresh lime juice
$1\frac{1}{2}$ tablespoons sour cream or crème fraîche
2 tablespoons chopped fresh basil

1   Cut melon in half and discard seeds. Scoop out flesh. Chop enough melon into small pieces to measure $\frac{1}{2}$ cup and reserve.

2   In 2 batches, puree large pieces of melon in a blender or food processor until smooth, about 30 seconds. Transfer to a bowl. Stir in lime juice and season with salt and pepper to taste. Stir in chopped melon and chill.

3   Stir soup, then ladle into bowls. Garnish with sour cream and basil.

4 SERVINGS

SIMPLE TIP *Stir the sour cream or crème fraîche first so that it liquefies slightly. Then it can be drizzled attractively over each serving.*

DRESS IT UP *Stir a splash of dry Spanish sherry into the soup for extra sophistication. Scattering a few red or green grape halves over each bowlful along with the basil is another nice touch.*

Sizzling Mushroom Soup

Plump, meaty mushrooms with their rich, earthy taste make this a great soup to start a chilly night's supper. And how does it get its name? A splash of hot olive oil and garlic hits the soup with a sizzle when it's poured in at the end. The recipe makes four good cupfuls, but if you'd prefer big bowls, simply double the amounts.

3 tablespoons olive oil

1 medium onion, chopped

10 ounces white button mushrooms, chopped

1$^1\!/_2$ tablespoons flour

$^1\!/_3$ cup canned crushed tomatoes

1 can (14$^1\!/_2$ ounces) chicken broth

1 garlic clove, minced

1 Heat 2 tablespoons of olive oil in a large saucepan over medium-high heat. Add onion and mushrooms. Cook, stirring occasionally, until mushrooms give off their liquid, 3 to 5 minutes.

2 Add flour and cook 1 minute, stirring. Stir in tomatoes, then broth. Simmer until onion is tender, about 10 minutes. Season with salt and pepper to taste. Keep hot.

3 Heat remaining 1 tablespoon oil in a small skillet over low heat. Add garlic and cook, stirring, until light gold, about 1 minute. Immediately pour into hot soup, stir, and serve.

4 SERVINGS

SIMPLE TIP *Want the soup a little creamy in texture? Puree ²/₃ cup of the finished soup in a blender and stir it into the rest.*

DRESS IT UP *Add a dollop of sour cream or crème fraîche and sprinkle each serving with fresh thyme leaves or chopped basil.*

VARIATION *For a vegetarian version, use vegetable broth in place of the chicken broth.*

Caramelized Onion and Garlic Soup

Lighter, faster, and easier than the classic cheese-topped French onion soup, this potful of meltingly tender onions and garlic in broth has its own kind of irresistibility, and an unexpected trick up its sleeve: Just before serving, an egg mixed with a little vinegar is stirred in. What happens is this: The soup takes on a slight creaminess from the egg and a bit of sparkle from the vinegar, making the whole deal that much more appealing. The recipe makes enough for 4 small bowls, but it can be doubled easily.

3 tablespoons butter
2 large onions, thinly sliced
5 large garlic cloves, thinly sliced
1 can (14$\frac{1}{2}$ ounces) chicken broth
1 large egg
1$\frac{1}{4}$ teaspoons white wine vinegar
4 slices French bread, $\frac{1}{2}$ inch thick, toasted

1   Melt 2 tablespoons of butter in a large saucepan over medium heat. Add onions and garlic. Cook, stirring frequently, until golden brown and tender, 10 to 12 minutes. Add broth plus $1/2$ cup water and simmer 10 minutes.

2   Lightly beat egg with vinegar in a small bowl. Spread remaining 1 tablespoon butter over one side of each slice of toast. Set a toast in each bowl.

3   Season soup with salt to taste, then remove from heat. Slowly whisk $1/4$ cup hot broth into egg mixture. Then gradually stir back into soup. Ladle into bowls, grind pepper over each, and serve.

4 SERVINGS

SIMPLE TIP *As the onions and garlic cook, they leave a savory brown residue on the sides and bottom of the pot. So when you add the liquids, be sure to stir the bottom and scrape the sides of the pan with a wooden spoon to incorporate these flavorful bits into the soup.*

Green Pea Soup

This soup is full of the taste of spring. And for me, its vibrant color is the fresh green of a lovely garden.

3 scallions
1$\frac{1}{2}$ cups chicken broth
1 box (10 ounces) frozen green peas
1$\frac{1}{2}$ tablespoons butter
Pinch of grated nutmeg
$\frac{1}{8}$ teaspoon dried dill

1 Thinly slice white and light green parts of scallions. Reserve dark green for another use.

2 Bring broth, frozen peas, and scallions to a boil in a large saucepan over high heat. Immediately reduce heat to medium and add butter. Simmer until peas are tender, 3 to 4 minutes.

3 Puree half at a time in a blender until smooth. Return to saucepan and season with salt and pepper to taste. Stir in nutmeg and dill. Reheat over low heat, if necessary. Serve hot.

3 TO 4 SERVINGS

SIMPLE TIPS *The soup is good served chilled in the summertime, too. But it thickens when it's cold, so thin it with a little broth or water.*

Keep the soup's bright green color when serving it chilled by cooling it rapidly in a bowl of ice water, stirring once in a while.

DRESS IT UP *Scatter buttery, crunchy croutons or crisp, crumbled bacon over the soup when it's served hot. And when hot or chilled, a drizzle of crème fraîche or sour cream is nice.*

Chunky Potato Soup in a Skillet

This may not be your usual way of making soup, but it's a fun way. Here's how: Potatoes and onion are cooked in water and olive oil in a deep skillet until the pan is dry and the potatoes are tender. Then the onion starts to color in the pan. So when the broth is added at the end, the liquid soaks up the browned onion flavor. The result is a rustic, homey soup for cold nights.

1 pound boiling potatoes
1 medium onion, thinly sliced
2 $1/2$ tablespoons olive oil
1 can (14 $1/2$ ounces) chicken broth
Big pinch of garlic powder
1 tablespoon chopped parsley

1 Peel potatoes and cut crosswise into slices $1/2$ inch thick. Place potatoes, onion, and olive oil in a deep 9- to 10-inch skillet. Cover with water by about $1/4$ inch. Bring to a boil over high heat.

2   Boil until water is gone, 15 to 20 minutes. Continue to cook until onion browns lightly, about 2 minutes, scraping skillet with a spatula to free brown bits. Reduce heat to low and chop potatoes with spatula.

3   Stir in broth and simmer 5 minutes. Season with garlic powder and salt and pepper to taste. Serve hot, sprinkled with parsley.

4 SERVINGS

DRESS IT UP *Cook 2 or 3 slices of bacon in the pan first, to use crumbled as a garnish. Use the rendered fat for part of the oil. Sprinkle each serving with fresh chives or scallion green.*

Roasted Mushroom and Zucchini Soup

When it's cold outside, I make this soup in the oven. When it's not and I don't want to heat up the kitchen, I accomplish the same thing by cooking the vegetables in a big, deep skillet over high heat until their juices flow. Then they simmer in broth for a minute or two. Whichever method you choose, what you end up with is a soup filled with meaty mushrooms and zucchini in rich tomato broth.

2 medium zucchini

10 ounces white button mushrooms

$1/3$ cup olive oil

2 large garlic cloves, chopped

2 tablespoons tomato paste

$1^1/3$ cups chicken broth

1   Preheat oven to 425°F. Chop zucchini and mushrooms into $3/4$-inch pieces. Toss with olive oil and garlic in a large bowl.

2   Roast in a 9-by-12-inch baking pan just until juices flow, 8 to 10 minutes. Stir in tomato paste and broth.

3 Cook in oven until broth is hot, 3 to 5 minutes. Season with salt and pepper to taste.

4 SERVINGS

SIMPLE TIP *If the vegetables are roasted in a very large pan, their liquid will evaporate quickly. If you find it has cooked away, add a little more broth or water at the end to compensate.*

Pasta

and

Noodles

Creamy No-Bake Macaroni and Cheese

Macaroni and cheese is a personal thing. Just ask any mom or dad with small children. The crucial part, I think, is having tons of cheese in a creamy sauce. And for me, I go with a meaty macaroni like shells over elbows. There's more to get your teeth into.

9 tablespoons butter
$^1/_2$ cup plain dry bread crumbs
$^1/_2$ cup grated Romano cheese
$^1/_3$ cup flour
5 cups milk
3 cups shredded extra-sharp Cheddar cheese
1 pound pasta shells or elbow macaroni

1 Bring a large pot of salted water to a boil for the pasta. Melt 4 tablespoons butter in a medium skillet over low heat. Stir in bread crumbs and cook, stirring, until golden brown, 2 to 3 minutes. Let cool, then toss with $^1/_4$ cup Romano cheese.

2 Melt remaining 5 tablespoons butter in a large saucepan over low heat. Whisk in flour and cook, stirring, 2 minutes. Gradually stir in milk. Mixture will be

very thick at first, then become thin. Bring to a low boil, stirring, to make a smooth sauce. Simmer, stirring frequently, 10 minutes. Remove from heat. Stir in Cheddar and remaining $1/4$ cup Romano cheese.

3   Boil pasta until just tender, about 6 minutes. Drain, then return to pot over low heat. Add cheese sauce and heat, stirring, 30 seconds. Season with salt and pepper. Transfer to a serving dish and sprinkle Romano crumbs over top. Serve hot.

6 SERVINGS

SIMPLE TIP *As the sauce cooks, some of the butter-flour thickening gets stuck in the corners of the pot. Go around with a spoon to stir it in.*

SERVING SUGGESTIONS *A romaine salad with tomatoes, cucumber, and garlic vinaigrette or Balsamic Caesar Salad (page 172) without the cheese. Or buttered green peas or spinach.*

Linguine with Frizzled Ham and Black Pepper

Regular sliced ham from the supermarket takes on new character when cut into strips and sautéed until brown and chewy. When it's tossed with linguine and enough freshly ground pepper to add a bit of a bite, you might be surprised at how something so simple can be so good.

1 pound linguine
$^1/_2$ pound thinly sliced ham
6 tablespoons butter
$^1/_3$ cup grated Parmesan cheese

1   Bring a large pot of salted water to a boil. Cook pasta until al dente, 8 to 10 minutes.

2   Meanwhile, cut ham into strips about $^1/_2$ inch wide and $1^1/_2$ inches long. Melt butter in a large skillet over high heat. Add ham. Cook, stirring occasionally, until strips curl and edges are well browned, 2 to 3 minutes.

3 Drain pasta, then return to pot. Add ham and butter. Cook over low heat, tossing and stirring, 30 to 60 seconds. Season with salt and pepper. Serve hot, with grated Parmesan cheese on top.

4 TO 6 SERVINGS

SIMPLE TIP *Toss the pasta and ham with a large wooden kitchen fork or tongs.*

SERVING SUGGESTIONS *A mesclun or watercress salad or Roast Tomatoes Provençal (page 140). And good bread, of course.*

DRESS IT UP *Stir 1 cup heavy cream into the pasta after the ham goes in. Heat them all together for a minute or so until the cream thickens a little.*

Baked Pennoni with Red Peppers and Parmesan Cheese

What's pennoni? I'd never heard of it until I saw a bag filled with what looked like fat penne. Well, that's what it is. And it's a terrific shape because the wider spaces trap more sauce. If your market doesn't carry this thick tubular pasta, mini rigatoni are good, or stick with regular penne. In this dish, the pennoni are tossed with tomatoes and sweet peppers, then baked under a blanket of grated Parmesan. When the dish emerges, the melted cheese gilds the top and adds rich, mellow flavor.

2 tablespoons butter

$^2/_3$ cup grated Parmesan cheese

1 medium red bell pepper, thinly sliced

1 $^3/_4$ cups crushed canned tomatoes in puree

8 ounces pennoni or other short, tubular pasta

1 Preheat oven to 450°F with a rack at the top. Bring a large pot of salted water to a boil for the pasta. Butter a shallow 8- to 9-inch round baking dish with 1 teaspoon butter. Sprinkle 2 tablespoons of Parmesan cheese over bottom and sides of dish.

2   Melt 1 tablespoon of butter in a medium saucepan over medium heat. Add bell pepper and sauté, stirring occasionally, 2 minutes. Add tomatoes and simmer over low heat, stirring occasionally, 5 minutes. The sauce should be thickened and pepper somewhat crisp. Season with salt and pepper.

3   Cook pasta until al dente, about 10 minutes. Drain and return to cooking pot. Toss with sauce. Spread in prepared dish. Cover top with remaining cheese and dot with remaining 2 teaspoons butter. Bake until outside is bubbling, cheese is melted, and pasta edges nicely browned. Serve hot.

3 TO 4 SERVINGS

SIMPLE TIP *The brand of canned crushed tomatoes with the richest flavor that I've found is Muir Glen. It has lots of sweet pieces of tomato in a light puree seasoned with a good deal of dried basil, perfect for this recipe.*

SERVING SUGGESTIONS *Sautéed broccoli rabe in garlic and oil or Stir-Fried Broccoli with Garlic (page 126). Crisp seeded Italian bread.*

Rigatoni in Creamy Artichoke Sauce

Artichoke hearts cooked in milk infuse the milk with their subtle, almost smoky flavor as they're turning tender. Pureed together, they become a luxurious sauce for pasta with a little help from Provolone cheese.

1 box (9 ounces) frozen artichoke hearts
$2^1/_2$ cups milk
1 tablespoon butter
1 pound rigatoni
1 cup shredded sharp Provolone cheese
$^1/_4$ cup chopped parsley

1 Bring frozen artichokes and milk to a simmer in a medium saucepan over low heat. Add butter and cook artichokes until tender, 5 to 6 minutes.

2 Transfer artichokes and 1 cup milk to a blender. Puree until almost smooth, 15 to 30 seconds. Stir back into remaining milk in saucepan. Season with salt and pepper. Remove artichoke sauce from heat and cover to keep warm.

3 In a large pot of salted boiling water, cook pasta until al dente, about 11 minutes. Drain, then return to pot over low heat. Stir in sauce and heat 30 to 60 seconds, stirring. Remove from heat and stir in cheese and parsley. Serve hot.

4 TO 6 SERVINGS

SIMPLE TIP *Set aside a little of the pasta cooking water. If the finished pasta seems thick, use the water to thin it down.*

SERVING SUGGESTIONS *Tossed green salad or tomatoes vinaigrette and crusty bread.*

DRESS IT UP *To add pretty orange color and extra appeal, scatter the top of each serving with skinny little strips of cooked carrots.*

Shells with Fresh Tomato and Garlic Oil

When you simmer garlic cloves and little grape tomatoes in olive oil, they happily impart their flavor to the oil. And when they are tossed with pasta and "salty and sharp" Romano cheese, this becomes a delicious dinner.

$2/3$ cup extra-virgin olive oil

8 large garlic cloves, lightly crushed

2 pints grape or cherry tomatoes

1 pound medium shells or mini rigatoni

$1/2$ cup grated Romano cheese

1   Heat olive oil in a large skillet over medium-low heat. Add garlic, and cook, turning occasionally, until golden, about 5 minutes. Stir in tomatoes and cook, stirring occasionally, until they collapse, about 5 minutes. Discard garlic. Remove pan from heat.

2   In a large pot of salted boiling water, cook pasta until al dente, about 5 minutes. Reserve $1/2$ cup cooking water, then drain pasta and return to pot over low heat.

Chilled Melon Soup with Fresh Basil *page 12*

Baked Pennoni with
Red Peppers and
Parmesan Cheese
page 30

Grilled Salmon with Lemon Hoisin Sauce *page 54*

Barbecued Shrimp *page 58*,
shown on Sautéed Corn and
Red Pepper Salad *page 182*

Chicken Breasts with Roasted Peppers,
Purple Olives, and Garlic *page 70*

Waldorf Chicken Legs *page 86*, shown with Smashed Potatoes with Scallions *page 158*

Turkey and Snow
Pea Stir-Fry *page 94*

Grilled Steak Fajitas with
Ancho Chile Salsa *page 100*

Cuban Pork Chops *page 120*

Roasted Asparagus with Parmesan Crumbs *page 124*

Savory Cheddar Cheese Muffins *page 150*

Smoked Chicken and Mango Salad *page 176*

Red Lettuce with Red Fruit in Cream Dressing *page 184*

Roasted Fresh Apricots
with Crème Fraiche *page 194*

Chocolate Cupcakes *page 198*

Raspberries with Butterscotch Cream *page 210*

3 Stir in tomatoes and reserved cooking water. Heat, stirring, 30 seconds. Stir in grated cheese. Season generously with salt and pepper. Grind a little more pepper over each serving.

4 TO 6 SERVINGS

SIMPLE TIP *The easiest way to peel garlic is to first lightly crush the clove with the side of a large knife. Then the skin slips right off.*

SERVING SUGGESTIONS *Any green salad is right, of course, but you could serve the Roasted Asparagus with Parmesan Crumbs (page 124) instead.*

VARIATION *For an additional note of flavor, stir a tablespoon of drained capers into the pasta right before serving.*

Green Fettuccine with Chicken and Two Cheeses

If you're in the mood for a creamy pasta, how about this one? It tastes as rich as a dish made with cream, but here ricotta cheese and egg yolk do the job. Fresh spinach fettuccine is cooked for seconds, just to soften the strands. Then the pasta is tossed with the other ingredients and sent off to bake in the oven, which cooks the chicken and crisps the top.

1 cup ricotta cheese

1 large egg yolk

$1/2$ cup grated Romano cheese

7 ounces skinless, boneless chicken breast

2 tablespoons butter

1 medium onion, chopped

9 ounces fresh spinach fettuccine

1 Preheat oven to 425°F. Bring a large pot of salted water to a boil. Meanwhile, beat ricotta and egg yolk in a medium bowl with a spoon for 30 seconds. Reserve 2 tablespoons of Romano; add remainder to ricotta mixture. Stir in $1/3$ cup water. Season with salt and pepper to taste.

2   Cut chicken in half lengthwise. Then cut crosswise into $1/2$-inch-wide strips. Melt $1^1/2$ tablespoons butter in a medium skillet over low heat. Add onion and cook, stirring occasionally, until tender but not brown, about 5 minutes. Stir in chicken, then remove from heat; the chicken will be mostly raw. Lightly oil a shallow 8- to 9-inch round baking dish.

3   Add pasta to boiling water and cook until it softens slightly, 15 to 30 seconds. Drain and return to pot. Toss with onion, chicken, and ricotta mixture. Spread in dish. Sprinkle with reserved Romano and dot with remaining $1^1/2$ teaspoons butter. Bake until top is tipped with brown and edges are bubbling, 12 to 15 minutes. Serve hot, cut into wedges.

4 SERVINGS

SERVING SUGGESTIONS *A bitter lettuce salad with arugula, watercress, radicchio, or endive tossed with balsamic vinegar and olive oil. Bread sticks, too.*

DRESS IT UP *Smaller wedges make a good first course for a special dinner. You can serve them as is, or make the dish without chicken and garnish the tops with strips of prosciutto when serving.*

Cheese Ravioli with Mushrooms and Parmesan Cheese

I love these ravioli in their mellow sauce of mushrooms, butter, and good Parmesan cheese, although it's not so much a sauce, really, as lightly thickened mushroom juices, which coat the pasta. Either way, when you cut into a ravioli, the cheese oozes into the juices and adds to the pleasure.

5 tablespoons butter
1 pound white button mushrooms
1 pound large cheese ravioli
$1/3$ cup grated Parmesan cheese
1 tablespoon chopped parsley

1   Bring a large pot of salted water to a boil for the ravioli. Soften 3 tablespoons of butter.

2   Melt remaining 2 tablespoons butter in a large skillet over medium heat. Add mushrooms and season with salt to taste. Cook, stirring occasionally, until juices flow, about 3 minutes. Remove from heat.

3   Boil ravioli until al dente, about 5 minutes. Drain, then return to pot over low heat. Toss with mushrooms and juices. Remove from heat and toss with softened butter and grated cheese. Season with pepper. Serve hot, with parsley sprinkled on top.

4 SERVINGS

SERVING SUGGESTIONS *Steamed broccoli, Lemon-Caper Carrots (page 128), or an arugula salad with tomatoes and warm, crusty bread.*

VARIATION *For an herbal note, add a little dried oregano or thyme when you toss the ravioli with the softened butter.*

Spaghetti with Port Wine Marinara Sauce

The small amount of Port added to the marinara sauce here is what I call "an invisible helper," which means it sweetens and intensifies the tomatoes while adding only a whisper of itself. After that, all the pasta needs is a sprinkle of good grated Parmesan before you plunge in your fork.

3 garlic cloves
1$\frac{1}{2}$ tablespoons extra-virgin olive oil
1$\frac{1}{2}$ tablespoons tomato paste
$\frac{1}{4}$ cup tawny Port
1 can (28 ounces) crushed tomatoes in puree
1 pound spaghetti

1 Cut garlic into thin lengthwise slices. Heat olive oil in a large saucepan over low heat. Add garlic and cook until pale gold, stirring, 2 minutes.

2 Stir in tomato paste; cook 15 seconds, then add Port. Add tomatoes and simmer, stirring occasionally, until sauce is thickened, about 15 minutes. Season with salt and pepper.

3 Meanwhile, bring a large pot of salted water to a boil. Add pasta and cook until al dente, 10 to 12 minutes. Drain, then return to pot over low heat. Add ½ cup sauce and heat 30 to 60 seconds, stirring. Serve spaghetti topped with more sauce and another grinding of pepper.

4 TO 6 SERVINGS

SIMPLE TIP *There are big differences among brands of canned crushed tomatoes. The best are simply pieces of tomato in juices or puree. Avoid those that list the word "concentrate." They won't have much, if any, texture.*

SERVING SUGGESTIONS *Arugula salad or broccoli sautéed in olive oil. Herb or onion focaccia.*

DRESS IT UP *Scatter a tablespoon or two of diced fresh mozzarella over each plate of pasta.*

VARIATION *Use dry Marsala instead of Port.*

Thai-Style Rice Noodles with Peanuts and Scallions

Rice noodles have a resilient, almost elastic quality, which makes them satisfying and fun to eat. In this recipe, just-cooked noodles get cooked for another minute or so in rich, spicy seasonings. Then you shower them with crunchy peanuts and scallions and dig in. This makes a great vegetarian lunch or light supper.

2 tablespoons rice vinegar
$1/2$ teaspoon Thai red curry paste
1 teaspoon finely chopped fresh ginger
$1/2$ cup soy sauce
$1/2$ cup vegetable oil
1 pound very thin rice sticks (*py mai fun*)
4 large scallions, thinly sliced
$1/3$ cup salted roast peanuts

1   In a small bowl, whisk together vinegar and curry paste. Stir in ginger, soy sauce, and oil. Season with $1/2$ teaspoon each salt and pepper. Set sauce aside.

2 Bring a large pot of water to a boil. Add noodles, and cook until chewy-tender, about 2 minutes. Drain well.

3 Pour sauce into a wok or very large skillet over low heat. Add noodles and half of scallions. Lift and toss with tongs until all strands are darkened with sauce, about 2 minutes. Serve hot or at room temperature, garnished with peanuts and remaining scallions.

4 SERVINGS

SERVING SUGGESTIONS *Stir-fried snap peas with carrots or Stir-Fried Broccoli with Garlic (page 126).*

DRESS IT UP *Scatter cilantro leaves and fresh basil over the noodles along with the scallions and peanuts.*

Chinese-Style Fresh Noodles with Pork

Egg pasta from the refrigerated section of the supermarket makes a good substitute for fresh Chinese noodles. Its toothy character can stand up to a gingery, garlicky sauce like this one. When I serve the noodles, I set bottles of soy sauce and sesame oil on the table, too. That way everyone can get into the act and dress up his own.

1 piece fresh ginger about 1 $\frac{1}{2}$ inches long

2 large scallions

4 large garlic cloves

2 tablespoons vegetable oil

$\frac{3}{4}$ pound ground pork

$\frac{1}{4}$ cup plus 2 tablespoons Chinese hoisin sauce

1 pound fresh thin egg noodles or linguine

1 Peel and finely chop ginger. Thinly slice scallions. Finely mince garlic.

2 Heat oil in a large skillet over low heat. Add garlic and ginger and cook, stirring, 30 seconds. Add ground pork, breaking it up with a large spoon. Cook until meat is no longer pink, 2 to 3 minutes. Stir in hoisin sauce and 1 $\frac{1}{3}$ cups

water. Simmer, stirring occasionally, until sauce is thickened, 4 to 5 minutes. Season with salt and pepper.

3   In a large pot of salted boiling water, cook noodles until al dente, about 3 minutes. Drain, then return to pot over low heat. Toss with scallions and half of sauce. Serve hot, topped with remaining sauce.

4 SERVINGS

SIMPLE TIP *Chop fresh ginger the Chinese way. First, cut off and peel a section. Slice it thinly across the grain. Lay the slices in a row between sheets of plastic wrap. Then pound them with a meat mallet, side of a cleaver, or bottom of a small skillet. They'll break up into tiny pieces.*

SERVING SUGGESTION *Crisp stir-fried snow peas or broccoli, or bok choy with mushrooms.*

Fish Fillets and Shrimp

Lemon and Lime—Crusted Cod

Cod and scrod (young cod) are mild, sweet-tasting fish, best, I think, when simply prepared. These fillets are spread with softened butter full of citrus zest and a smidgen of bread crumbs. When they're broiled, the top turns lightly crisp, almost the color of sunshine.

6 tablespoons butter, softened
1 1/2 teaspoons grated lemon zest
1 1/2 teaspoons grated lime zest
1 tablespoon plain dry bread crumbs
4 cod fillets, 7 ounces each, cut 1 inch thick

1   Preheat broiler with rack about 5 inches from the heat. In a medium bowl, combine butter, lemon zest, and lime zest. Stir in bread crumbs. Season with 1/4 teaspoon each salt and pepper.

2   Lay fillets in an oiled broiling pan and season lightly with salt. Spread flavored butter over fish.

3 Broil without turning until fillets are just cooked through and tops are golden, 6 to 7 minutes. Serve hot.

4 SERVINGS

SIMPLE TIPS *Hake, haddock, and halibut are fine substitutes for cod, which is good to know if you live on the East Coast, where North Atlantic cod has been seriously depleted. Alaskan cod, however, is still plentiful.*

Dry the fillets on paper towels first. It helps the butter to adhere. And speaking of butter, unsalted is what I use. Season a little lighter if you use the salted kind.

SERVING SUGGESTIONS *Glazed carrots or Sautéed Grape Tomatoes, Chicago Style (page 142) and boiled potatoes with fresh dill or Browned Onion Rice Pilaf (page 164).*

Halibut with Creamy Dill Butter

This is my favorite way of preparing halibut fillets. First, I dip them into bread crumbs. Their natural moisture lets the lightest coating adhere. Then I brown them in a pan until golden and pop them into the oven for the last few minutes of cooking. They're served with a delicate, simple topping of dill butter and sour cream. Preparation couldn't be simpler—or more understated and elegant.

3 tablespoons butter, softened
$^3/_4$ teaspoon dried dill
3 tablespoons sour cream
4 skinless halibut fillets, 7 ounces each, cut 1 inch thick
$^1/_3$ cup plain dry bread crumbs
$1^1/_2$ tablespoons vegetable oil

1 Preheat oven to 375°F. Combine butter and dill in a small bowl. Mix in sour cream until as smooth as possible. Season lightly with salt and pepper.

2 Sprinkle halibut fillets with salt and pepper. Dip both sides into crumbs, pressing lightly to adhere.

3 Heat oil in a large, ovenproof skillet over medium-high heat. Add fish rounded side down and cook until golden, about 3 minutes, Turn over, then transfer skillet to oven. Bake until just cooked through, 4 to 5 minutes. Serve hot, topped with a dollop of dill butter.

4 SERVINGS

SIMPLE TIP *The rounded side of the fillet is the prettiest side. That's why you brown it first. So when the fish is ready to serve, it's the side you'll see on the plate.*

SERVING SUGGESTIONS *Asparagus or Wilted Green Beans with Red Onion (page 136). Boiled new potatoes or Tomato Couscous (page 168).*

VARIATION *The creamy dill butter is good with other mild white-fleshed fish such as sole and cod.*

Steamed Mussels with Scallion-Parsley Pesto

Scallions and parsley tossed into a food processor with garlic and olive oil make a zesty blend for seasoning these mussels. The pesto does its work in two ways: Half is stirred into the cooked broth to deepen the flavor; then the rest is spooned into empty shells to become a condiment with which to dab each morsel. Cultivated mussels make this dish easy and quick to prepare.

1 large bunch flat-leaf parsley
6 scallions, white and light green parts only, thinly sliced
3 garlic cloves, thinly sliced
$1/4$ cup extra-virgin olive oil
4 pounds cultivated mussels

1 Cut parsley bunch just below leaves. Discard stems. Measure $1^1/_2$ lightly packed cups leaves, removing stray stems. Wash and drain well. Finely chop parsley, scallions, and garlic with olive oil in a food processor, pulsing until almost a paste, 1 to 2 minutes. Season with salt to taste.

2 Rinse mussels and drain well. If any have wiry beards, snip off with a scissors.

Place mussels and $1/4$ cup water in a very large pot over high heat. Cover and cook just until shells open, 4 to 6 minutes. With a slotted skimmer or large spoon, transfer mussels to bowls, leaving broth in pot over low heat.

3   Choose 4 large mussels and separate halves, adding meat to bowls. Fill shell halves with half the pesto. Stir remaining pesto into broth. Season generously with pepper. Ladle over mussels. Serve hot, with 2 pesto-filled shells atop each serving.

4 SERVINGS

SIMPLE TIP *The mussels cool quickly once they're out of the pot. If they're served in ovenproof bowls, they can be slipped into a low oven while you finish the dish.*

SERVING SUGGESTIONS *Corn on the cob grilled or roasted in a very hot oven. Or Grilled Zucchini with Balsamic Dressing (page 144). Good bread for sopping up the juices.*

Grilled Salmon with Lemon Hoisin Sauce

No other fish can quite match the succulence of salmon from the grill. Over fire, the pink fillets take on beautiful golden color and turn wonderfully crisp. If you remove them from the heat just before they are completely cooked through— slightly pearly in the center—you'll find the fish especially luscious and moist. In this recipe, the salmon is served on a bed of cool, crunchy bean sprouts and cucumber slices. A generous drizzle of punchy sauce pulls together all the contrasts of taste, texture, and temperature.

1 Kirby cucumber

3 tablespoons Chinese hoisin sauce

$\frac{1}{4}$ cup fresh lemon juice

4 skinless salmon fillets, 7 ounces each, cut 1 inch thick

$1\frac{1}{3}$ cups mung bean sprouts

1 Prepare a medium-hot fire in a barbecue grill. Peel and thinly slice cucumber. Stir hoisin sauce and lemon juice together in a small bowl.

2 Season salmon fillets with salt and grill, rounded side down, until brown, 5 to 6 minutes. Turn over and grill until almost cooked through, 3 to 4 minutes, or to taste.

3 Lay cucumber on plates, then cover with a low mound of bean sprouts. Drizzle with lemon hoisin sauce. Top with a salmon fillet. Drizzle on a little more sauce and finish with a grinding of pepper each. Serve right away.

4 SERVINGS

SIMPLE TIPS *As long as the grill rack is hot and brushed with oil right before cooking, the salmon doesn't need to be oiled because of its high fat content. Also, let the fillets form a crust before trying to move them. Then they won't stick.*

If your fillets have skin, it's easy to remove it after cooking. It peels right off.

SERVING SUGGESTIONS *Grilled multicolored bell peppers. Along with grilled potatoes, Asian noodles in a little broth with drops of sesame oil, or Sesame Pitas (page 154).*

Roasted Salmon with Curry Sauce

The restaurant trick of browning fish fillets on top of the stove and then finishing them in the oven is a great technique, because they cook to perfection in the all-around heat. Here, salmon is cooked just that way, then topped with a lightly curried, slightly spicy sour cream.

1/4 cup sour cream

1 teaspoon curry powder

2 tablespoons fresh lemon juice

1 tablespoon mango chutney

4 salmon fillets, 7 ounces each, cut 1 inch thick

1 tablespoon vegetable oil

1   Preheat oven to 400°F. Place sour cream in a small bowl. Stir in curry powder, lemon juice, and chutney. Season with salt and pepper to taste.

2   Dry fillets with paper towels. Season with salt and pepper. Heat oil in a large ovenproof skillet over high heat. Add fillets rounded side down and sauté until golden on the bottom, 2 to 3 minutes. Turn fish over and transfer skillet to oven.

3 Roast until salmon is almost cooked through, 6 to 7 minutes, or to taste. Serve hot, with a dollop of sauce on top.

4 SERVINGS

SERVING SUGGESTIONS *Green Beans with Nutmeg and Lemon (page 135) or Sautéed Grape Tomatoes, Chicago Style (page 142). Rice or warmed pita breads brushed with olive oil.*

VARIATION *Replace the chutney with about a teaspoon of finely chopped fresh ginger. And if you prefer mayonnaise over sour cream, you can substitute it in the same proportion.*

Barbecued Shrimp

Shrimp are so good. They take to all sorts of seasonings and cook in mere minutes. And when grilled, they char just a bit and pick up a touch of smoky flavor. In this recipe, the shrimp are cooked in a light and peppery marinade, which leaves a gentle glow in your mouth.

2 tablespoons ketchup
2 tablespoons soy sauce
2 tablespoons fresh lemon juice
1 tablespoon butter, melted
$1\frac{1}{2}$ pounds large shrimp, peeled and deveined

1 Prepare a hot fire in a barbecue grill. Combine ketchup, soy sauce, lemon juice, and melted butter in a small bowl. Season with $\frac{1}{8}$ teaspoon salt and 1 teaspoon freshly ground pepper.

2 Dry shrimp on paper towels. Thread onto skewers. Lay in a single layer on a baking sheet. Spoon sauce over and turn several times to coat. Marinate 10 minutes at room temperature.

3 Grill, turning once, until shrimp are cooked through and edges lightly charred, about 4 minutes. Serve hot.

4 SERVINGS

SIMPLE TIP *Shrimp designated as "large" can mean any-where from 21 to 30 pieces to a pound. So if you buy frozen, cleaned shrimp in a bag, it's safe to figure 8 good-sized shrimp per person.*

SERVING SUGGESTIONS *Grilled corn on the cob or Sautéed Corn and Red Pepper Salad (page 182) and Savory Cheddar Cheese Muffins (page 150).*

Garlic and Lime–Roasted Shrimp with Tomato

As my husband says, "This is a real midweek dish." And he means that in only the nicest way! To translate: It's quick to throw together (he watched me do it), fast to cook (he saw that, too), yet there is still something special about it. As far as taste goes, I think the name pretty much says it all.

1 1/2 pounds large shrimp, peeled and deveined
1 medium tomato
3 tablespoons extra-virgin olive oil
4 large garlic cloves, minced
3 tablespoons fresh lime juice

1   Preheat oven to 450°F. Dry shrimp on paper towels. Cut tomato into 8 wedges.

2   Place shrimp and tomato in a large bowl. Toss with olive oil, garlic, and half of lime juice. Season with salt to taste. Transfer to a shallow baking dish large enough to hold shrimp in a single layer.

3 Roast until shrimp are white throughout, about 8 minutes. Remove from oven and sprinkle remaining lime juice over shrimp. Add a very generous grinding of pepper and serve hot.

4 SERVINGS

SIMPLE TIP *For cooking the shrimp I use a copper gratin dish, which heats up fast. If you use a heavy baking dish, the cooking time will be a little longer.*

SERVING SUGGESTIONS *Sliced beets or Corn in Parmesan Garlic Cream (without the garlic; page 130), steamed rice or Rustic Onion Rolls (page 152).*

Shrimp in Ginger Coconut Cream

Ginger and coconut just might be soul mates for shrimp. Simply imagine them in a satiny sauce full of rich spice. As far as coconut milk is concerned, buy the regular kind, not the one labeled "lite"—and, of course, be sure it is unsweetened.

1$\frac{1}{2}$ pounds large shrimp, peeled and deveined
1 medium-to-large red bell pepper
1 tablespoon vegetable oil
1 tablespoon finely chopped fresh ginger
1 can (13$\frac{1}{2}$ ounces) coconut milk
Lime wedges

1   Dry shrimp on paper towels. Cut pepper into long, thin strips.

2   Heat oil in a large skillet over medium heat. Add pepper strips and ginger and cook, stirring, 30 seconds. Add shrimp and coconut milk. Cook, turning shrimp occasionally, until pink, curled, and white inside, about 3 minutes. With a slotted spoon, transfer shrimp and peppers to a bowl.

3 Increase heat to medium-high. Boil down sauce until thickened, stirring occasionally, and adding any shrimp juices from the bowl, 3 to 5 minutes. Season with salt and pepper. Remove sauce from heat. Stir shrimp and peppers back into sauce. Serve hot, with lime wedges on the side.

4 SERVINGS

SERVING SUGGESTIONS *Stir-fried sugar snap peas, snow peas, green beans. Steamed jasmine, basmati, or regular white rice.*

DRESS IT UP *Sprinkle each serving with chopped fresh cilantro and basil.*

VARIATION *Stir $^1/_4$ teaspoon Thai red curry paste into the sauce after reducing it.*

Sole with Lemon and Mustard Brown Butter

Delicate fillets of sole are baked before being dressed with their seasoned butter. The butter itself is a simple enough affair. It's cooked in a skillet with lemon juice until it turns light brown and tastes nutty. Then mustard is stirred in, which, along with the acid in the lemon, adds a good sharp note to cut the lushness of the fish.

4 sole fillets, 7 ounces each
$3^1/_2$ tablespoons butter
$^1/_4$ cup fresh lemon juice
1 tablespoon Dijon mustard

1   Preheat oven to 400°F. Fold under both ends of fillets to form 4 rectangular packets, each about $^3/_4$ inch thick.

2   Lay fish in a baking pan and dot with $1^1/_2$ teaspoons of butter. Season with salt and pepper. Bake until white throughout, about 10 minutes. Remove from oven.

3 Melt remaining butter with lemon juice in a medium skillet over high heat. Cook, swirling pan, until butter turns light brown, about 2 minutes. Remove from heat and whisk In mustard. It won't be smooth. Season lightly with salt and pepper. Spoon over fish and serve hot.

4 SERVINGS

SIMPLE TIP *The fillets throw off a good amount of liquid as they cook. Drain them before serving so the butter won't become diluted.*

SERVING SUGGESTIONS *Roasted Tomatoes Provençal (page 140). (Roast the tomatoes before the fish since they cook at a higher temperature. Serve them warm or reheat briefly.) And parslied new potatoes.*

VARIATION *Other white-fleshed fish, such as halibut and cod, make good substitutes for the sole.*

Grilled Swordfish Steaks with Cumin-Paprika Oil

This spiced oil has plenty of flavor. Just the right amount, in fact, to highlight the swordfish without overwhelming it. Be sure, though, that the spices you use haven't been sitting around for more than 6 months. Otherwise they are sure to have faded in intensity, and you'll have fish that turns a beautiful color on the grill but doesn't give much of a payoff in the mouth.

2 tablespoons extra-virgin olive oil
2 1/2 teaspoons ground cumin
2 teaspoons paprika
4 swordfish steaks, 7 ounces each, cut 1 inch thick

1   Prepare a medium-hot fire in a barbecue grill. Stir olive oil, cumin, and paprika together in a small bowl. Season generously with salt.

2   Place swordfish on a platter and spoon on oil. Spread over both sides with the back of a spoon. Marinate 10 minutes.

3 Grill first side until nicely browned, about 5 minutes. Turn over and grill until just cooked through, 4 to 5 minutes more. Finish with a grinding of pepper and serve hot.

4 SERVINGS

SIMPLE TIP *The marinated steaks can brown quickly on a hot grill. If that happens, turn and brown the second side, then finish the cooking on a cooler section of the grill.*

SERVING SUGGESTIONS *Sliced tomatoes with yogurt and mint dressing or Lemon-Caper Carrots (page 128). Grilled bread rubbed with garlic and olive oil or Silver Dollar Corn Cakes (page 148).*

Mostly

Boneless Birds

Chicken Breasts with Roasted Peppers, Purple Olives, and Garlic

The chicken, vegetables, and olive oil cook under cover over very low heat. This simple technique creates aromatic steam, which helps keep the chicken juicy. Meanwhile, the peppers, olives, garlic, and oil blend their flavors in a delicious, concentrated way.

12 pitted kalamata olives

$1/4$ cup extra-virgin olive oil

1 cup coarsely chopped roasted red bell peppers

2 large garlic cloves, thinly sliced

3 tablespoons tomato puree

4 skinless, boneless chicken breasts, 7 ounces each

1 Coarsely chop olives. Heat olive oil in a large skillet over low heat. Stir in roasted peppers, garlic, chopped olives, and tomato puree. Season with salt and $1/4$ teaspoon freshly ground pepper. Cook, stirring occasionally, 3 to 4 minutes.

2 Add chicken to skillet, cover pan, and reduce heat to as low as possible. Cook, turning once, until chicken is white throughout, about 8 minutes.

3 Serve chicken hot, with sauce spooned on top.

4 SERVINGS

SIMPLE TIP *The quality of prepared roasted peppers varies widely. Look for jars that contain vivid red peppers that appear firm and whole. Check the label to avoid ones that have citric acid listed. I buy the Peloponnese brand.*

SERVING SUGGESTIONS *Roasted or grilled summer squash or Balsamic Caesar Salad (page 172). Smashed Potatoes with Fresh Basil (page 158) or Tomato Couscous (page 168).*

VARIATION *Want to add a little heat to this dish? Sprinkle in a big pinch of hot pepper flakes as the chicken cooks.*

Grilled Chicken Kebabs in Rosemary Yogurt

Yogurt does lots of work here. First, it acts as a seasoning along with rosemary, lending its inimitable mild tang. Then it helps the meat to brown and remain moist during grilling. Finally, a spoonful on top sauces the kebabs when they're served. Use either metal or bamboo skewers, but be sure to soak the bamboo ones for about 30 minutes first so they don't burn.

4 skinless, boneless chicken breasts, 7 ounces each
$1/2$ cup plain yogurt
2 teaspoons extra-virgin olive oil
$2^1/2$ teaspoons dried rosemary

1   Prepare a medium fire in a barbecue grill. Cut chicken breasts lengthwise in half, then across into 1-inch pieces.

2   In a large bowl, season yogurt with olive oil, rosemary, $1/2$ teaspoon salt, and $1/4$ teaspoon freshly ground pepper. Set aside 3 tablespoons of rosemary yogurt to use as sauce. Add chicken to remaining yogurt and stir to coat all over. Thread chicken onto skewers.

3 Grill, turning to brown all sides, until chicken is white throughout, about 8 minutes. Slide meat off skewers onto plates. Serve with a dollop of rosemary yogurt on top.

4 SERVINGS

SIMPLE TIP *As you skewer the chicken, leave about $1/2$ inch between each piece. That way they'll cook more evenly. And be sure to brush the grill lightly with oil just before cooking.*

SERVING SUGGESTIONS *Grilled tomatoes and sliced beets or Grilled Zucchini with Balsamic Dressing (page 144). Sesame Pitas (page 154).*

DRESS IT UP *Alternate the chicken with pieces of red or green bell pepper. Or wind a strip of bacon around and between the chicken pieces as you skewer them.*

VARIATIONS *Grill the chicken breasts whole instead of turning them into kebabs.*

Use dill or oregano in place of the rosemary.

Chicken Burgers in Jamaican Jerk Sauce

Jerk sauce is great stuff. Its feisty pepper, onion, garlic, and vinegar flavor make plain-jane chicken burgers come alive. The brand I use is Vernon's Jamaican Jerk Sauce, which I pluck right off the supermarket shelf.

$1\frac{1}{2}$ pounds lean ground chicken
$\frac{1}{3}$ cup plain dry bread crumbs
$1\frac{1}{2}$ tablespoons vegetable oil
2 tablespoons Jamaican jerk sauce

1   With a fork, mix chicken in a large bowl with $\frac{3}{4}$ teaspoon salt. Form into 4 thick burgers. Press both sides into crumbs and flatten burgers to $\frac{3}{4}$ inch as you press.

2   Heat oil in a large nonstick skillet over medium heat. Add burgers and cook on one side until golden brown, about 3 minutes. Reduce heat to low, turn burgers over, and cook about 4 minutes, or until just cooked through. Transfer to plates.

3   Add jerk sauce and $^1/_2$ cup water to skillet. Reduce by half, stirring occasionally, about 3 minutes. Season sauce with salt to taste, spoon over burgers, and serve.

4 SERVINGS

SIMPLE TIP *If you moisten your hands with water before forming the burgers, the meat won't stick to your fingers.*

SERVING SUGGESTIONS *Spinach, chard, or other cooked greens. Silver Dollar Corn Cakes (page 148) or Sweet Potatoes with Creamy Orange-Thyme Butter (page 162).*

Grilled Chinese Flavor Chicken Cutlets

These cutlets are pounded thin so they can marinate in 10 minutes and grill in 5. Their taste is teriyaki-like but gentler, befitting a mild breast of chicken. Be sure not to overcook them so they'll be tender and juicy.

3 tablespoons fresh lemon juice

1 tablespoon soy sauce

$^3/_4$ teaspoon sugar

$^3/_4$ teaspoon sesame oil

4 skinless, boneless chicken breasts, 7 ounces each

1 Prepare a hot fire in a barbecue grill. Combine lemon juice, soy sauce, sugar, and sesame oil in a small bowl.

2 Lay chicken breasts between sheets of plastic wrap. Pound an even $^1/_4$ inch thickness with a meat mallet or back of a small skillet. Set on a platter and pour soy-lemon sauce over chicken. Turn to coat. Let marinate 10 minutes, turning several times.

3   Season chicken with salt and pepper. Grill first side until lightly browned, about 3 minutes. Turn over and grill 1 to 2 minutes more, until just cooked through. Serve hot.

4 SERVINGS

SIMPLE TIP Be sure the grill rack is hot and brushed with oil before grilling so the chicken doesn't stick.

SERVING SUGGESTIONS Cucumber salad, grilled asparagus, or Red Lettuce with Red Fruit in Cream Dressing (page 184). Grilled bell peppers cut into strips and served on top of buttered rice or Tomato Couscous (page 168).

Sautéed Chicken Provençale

For all fans of chicken on the bone (like me), here's one for you. Browned until crisp, then finished in the oven with tomatoes and herbs, this chicken dish has an unexpected element—paprika. Which turns the tomatoes a richer red, and more important, adds a special note of flavor. But if your paprika is older than six months, it's time for a new jar.

3 pounds cut-up chicken or chicken thighs
1 tablespoon extra-virgin olive oil
1 teaspoon paprika
$3/4$ cup canned crushed tomatoes in puree
$2^1/_2$ teaspoons dried herbes de Provence

1 Preheat oven to 400°F. Dry chicken on paper towels. Season generously with salt and pepper. Heat olive oil in a large ovenproof skillet over medium-high heat. In two batches, add chicken skin side down and sauté until golden and crusted, about 5 minutes. Turn and lightly brown other side, 2 minutes.

2 Remove skillet from heat, transfer chicken to platter, and pour off fat. Stir in paprika, tomatoes, and herbs, scraping up brown bits on the bottom. Return chicken to skillet.

3 Transfer to oven and bake, uncovered, until chicken is just cooked through, about 15 minutes. If sauce is thin, remove chicken and boil down briefly to concentrate. Serve chicken hot, with sauce on top.

4 SERVINGS

SIMPLE TIP *Cut the chicken breasts crosswise in half before you cook them. They're easier to handle, and it makes more servings of white meat.*

SERVING SUGGESTIONS *Sautéed or grilled yellow squash or Green Beans with Nutmeg and Lemon (page 135). Or a tossed salad with arugula. And garlic mashed potatoes.*

VARIATION *If you don't have any herbes de Provence, you can mix your own. Combine 1¼ teaspoons dried thyme with ¾ teaspoon dried rosemary, ¼ teaspoon dried marjoram, and ¼ teaspoon fennel seed.*

Crisp Chicken Cutlets with Honey Mustard

Sometimes all I want for dinner is a simple breaded chicken breast topped with something that adds plenty of zip. Here's one that's pounded thin so it can be quickly pan-fried in a shallow amount of oil. Just enough oil, in fact, to turn both sides crisp and golden simultaneously. I often see thinly sliced breasts for sale at the market, but it's also easy to pound thicker ones yourself.

4 skinless, boneless chicken breasts, 6 ounces each

2 eggs

$2/3$ cup plain dry bread crumbs

Vegetable oil, for frying

3 tablespoons prepared honey mustard (I use Honeycup)

1 Lay chicken breasts between sheets of plastic wrap. Pound an even $1/4$ inch thick with a meat mallet or back of a small skillet. Season with salt and pepper.

2 Lightly beat eggs with 3 tablespoons water. Dip both sides of chicken first into egg, then into bread crumbs, pressing to adhere. Lay in a single layer on a platter.

3 Heat oil to a depth of 1 inch in a large skillet over medium-low heat until a pinch of bread crumbs foams. Adding 1 or 2 at a time, cook chicken breasts without turning until golden, $1\frac{1}{2}$ to 2 minutes. Drain on paper towels. Serve hot, topped with a spoonful of honey mustard.

4 SERVINGS

SIMPLE TIP *It's best to fry only one or two cutlets at a time so the temperature of the oil stays consistent. Keep them warm in a low oven on a cake cooling rack on top of a baking sheet while doing the rest.*

SERVING SUGGESTIONS *Wilted Green Beans with Red Onion (page 136) or Slow-Sautéed Turnips (page 143). Mashed potatoes with browned onions or Smashed Potatoes with Fresh Basil (page 158).*

Pepper Chicken with Romano Cheese

The lightest coating of mustard, pungent Romano cheese, and freshly ground pepper gives sautéed chicken breasts a beautiful brown color and pleasingly sharp flavor. But first, the breasts are lightly pounded with a meat mallet or the back of a small skillet (or even the bottom of your fist) so they cook quickly and stay juicy.

1/3 cup freshly grated Romano cheese
4 skinless, boneless chicken breasts, 7 ounces each
2 teaspoons Dijon mustard
2 tablespoons olive oil

1   Mix cheese with 1/2 teaspoon freshly ground pepper. Set aside 4 teaspoons and place the rest on a plate.

2   Lay breasts between sheets of plastic wrap. Pound to an even 1/2 inch thickness with a meat mallet or back of a small skillet. Season with salt. Spread 1/2 teaspoon mustard over the top of each breast. Press both sides into peppered cheese to coat.

3 Heat olive oil in a large nonstick skillet over medium heat. When hot, add chicken breasts mustard side down and brown, about 2 minutes. Turn, and cook 2 minutes more. Transfer to plates, sprinkle each with 1 teaspoon cheese, and serve.

4 SERVINGS

SIMPLE TIP *Coat the chicken with cheese right before cooking. And make sure the oil in the pan is hot before adding them, so they don't stick.*

SERVING SUGGESTIONS *Buttered carrots, or Stir-Fried Broccoli with Garlic (page 126). Rice pilaf, or Sweet Potatoes with Creamy Orange-Thyme Butter (page 162).*

Grilled Chicken Sausage with Sweet Peppers and Mustard Sauce

I like chicken sausages best when they're grilled, because they brown beautifully all around and pick up extra character from the smoke. In this recipe, the juicy links are served nestled inside halves of grilled red peppers. Then the duo is sauced with a spoonful of sour cream kicked up with sharp mustard to tie their tastes together.

1$\frac{1}{4}$ teaspoons powdered mustard

1$\frac{1}{2}$ teaspoons red wine vinegar

$\frac{1}{3}$ cup sour cream

2 large red bell peppers

1$\frac{1}{2}$ teaspoons olive oil

1$\frac{3}{4}$ pounds raw chicken sausages

1 Prepare a medium-hot fire in a barbecue grill. Mix mustard with vinegar and 1 teaspoon water in a small bowl. Stir in sour cream. Season with salt and pepper. Cut peppers in half. Discard seeds and stems. Rub skins with oil.

2　　Place peppers skin side down on grill along with sausages. Cook sausages, turning to brown all around, until just cooked through, 8 to 10 minutes. Cook peppers until lightly charred. Then turn and cook until tender but still firm, about 8 minutes total.

3　　Set peppers on plates cavities up. Season each with a pinch of salt. Lay sausages in peppers. Spoon mustard sauce on top and serve.

4 SERVINGS

SIMPLE TIP *To help the peppers cook more evenly, make 2 or 3 small cuts on the ends of each pepper half. Then press down to flatten.*

SERVING SUGGESTIONS *Other grilled vegetables such as asparagus, sliced eggplant, tomato halves, or thick slices of red onion. Grilled new potatoes or Savory Noodle Pie (page 166).*

Waldorf Chicken Legs

When I was a chef at the Waldorf-Astoria, one of the staff meals was roasted chicken legs. The employee cafeteria cooks prepared more than a hundred at a time, often twice a week. Surprisingly, no matter how many times those legs appeared, I was never sorry to see them show up. They're simple good fare. And for us at home, they take only ten minutes of work; the oven does the rest. Here's my version.

2 teaspoons paprika

1$\frac{1}{2}$ teaspoons dried oregano

$\frac{1}{4}$ teaspoon garlic powder

4 large chicken legs, whole or separated into drumsticks and thighs

1 tablespoon Worcestershire sauce

1 tablespoon flour

1 Preheat oven to 425°F with rack at the top. Mix paprika, oregano, and garlic powder in a small bowl. Dry chicken legs with paper towels.

2 Arrange on a baking sheet in a single layer. Season generously with salt and pepper. Drizzle with Worcestershire sauce, rubbing it in lightly. Sprinkle sea-

soning mixture all over legs and pat on. Sprinkle flour over tops of chicken and pat gently to help adhere.

3 Roast chicken floured side up, basting once or twice with fat in pan, 30 minutes, or until nicely brown and tender. Serve hot.

4 SERVINGS

SERVING SUGGESTIONS *Tossed salad with sliced mushrooms and avocado or Sautéed Red Cabbage with Parmesan Cheese (page 134). Savory Noodle Pie (page 166) or buttered noodles.*

DRESS IT UP *Serve the legs with savory pan juices. Add ¼ cup water or wine to the baking pan and scrape up the browned bits. Pour the juices into a small bowl and spoon off the fat after it rises. Reheat the juices and serve them in a small pitcher on the side.*

Turkey Burgers with Hoisin Sauce

Chinese hoisin sauce is a somewhat sweet, distinctively rich flavoring you can find in jars in the Asian section of the supermarket. It's a convenient food to keep around and has tons of uses. For one, bland ground turkey gets a real boost when combined with just a few tablespoons of the stuff. And for two, it dresses these burgers to a "T" when mixed with soy sauce.

1$\frac{1}{2}$ tablespoons soy sauce

4$\frac{1}{2}$ tablespoons Chinese hoisin sauce

1$\frac{3}{4}$ pounds ground turkey

2 teaspoons grated fresh ginger

1 large garlic clove, minced

$\frac{1}{4}$ cup plain dry bread crumbs

1 tablespoon vegetable oil

1 Stir soy sauce into 2 tablespoons of hoisin sauce. Set sauce aside.

2 With a fork, mix ground turkey in a large bowl with the remaining hoisin,

ginger, garlic, $3/4$ teaspoon salt, and $1/4$ teaspoon fresh pepper. Form into 4 burgers $3/4$ inch thick. Press both sides into crumbs.

3 Heat oil in a large nonstick skillet over low heat. Add burgers. Cook, turning once, until browned and just cooked through, about 15 minutes. Serve hot, with sauce on top.

4 SERVINGS

SERVING SUGGESTIONS *Stir-fried carrots and Chinese cabbage or Sesame Edamame (page 132). Scallion couscous or Roasted Baked Potatoes (page 160). Or serve the burgers in buns with coleslaw.*

VARIATIONS *Meatloaf Burgers with Hoisin Sauce: Substitute $1 3/4$ pounds meatloaf mix (equal parts beef, pork, and veal) for the ground turkey.*

Try the hoisin and soy sauce with grilled shrimp, pork, or chicken.

Turkey Scallopine with Lemon Butter

Turkey cutlets can turn into skinny scallopine with a meat mallet or back of a small skillet and a small amount of effort. But instead of sautéing them as the big sheets they become, here they're folded into thirds before cooking, which fits a lot more in the pan.

6 turkey breast cutlets, 1^1/$_2$ pounds total
2 tablespoons fresh lemon juice
^{1}/$_4$ cup flour
2 tablespoons butter
^{1}/$_4$ teaspoon dried marjoram

1   Rinse cutlets and pat dry with paper towels. Place between sheets of plastic wrap and pound to an even ^{1}/$_8$ inch thickness.

2   Season with salt and pepper. Moisten tops on one side with 2 teaspoons of lemon juice and lightly rub in. Fold lengthwise into thirds, lemon side in, like a letter. Dredge both sides in flour and tap off excess.

3   Melt butter in a large nonstick skillet over medium-low heat. When it froths, add turkey scallopine and lightly brown one side, about 2 minutes. Turn over,

reduce heat to low, and lightly brown other side, about 2 more minutes. Continue to cook, turning once or twice, until golden brown and cooked through, 1 to 2 minutes. Remove skillet from heat and pour remaining lemon juice over turkey. Serve scallopine hot, drizzled with pan juices and sprinkled with marjoram.

4 SERVINGS

SIMPLE TIP *When you sauté in pure butter, the butter can burn. To avoid that, keep the heat low once the scallopine are browned and move them around in the pan as they cook. When they're done, the butter will be nutty brown and delicious.*

SERVING SUGGESTIONS *Steamed spinach, or Roasted Asparagus with Parmesan Crumbs (page 124). Warm, soft dinner rolls or Garden Mashed Potatoes (page 156).*

VARIATION *Lots of markets sell turkey breast in packages already cut for scallopine. In the ones I've seen, the pieces are uniformly thin but smaller. So make 8 pieces instead of 6.*

Grilled Turkey Roulades with Sun-Dried Tomatoes

Easy to assemble and quick to cook, these turkey roll-ups can be on the table in minutes. Simply grill them over a relatively low fire. That way they'll cook all the way through and still stay tender and juicy.

6 turkey breast cutlets, $1^1/_2$ pounds total
$^3/_4$ teaspoon dried oregano
6 slices Swiss cheese, about 1 ounce each
6 drained sun-dried tomato halves, oil reserved

1   Prepare a medium-low fire in a barbecue grill. Rinse cutlets and pat dry with paper towels. Season on one side with $^3/_4$ teaspoon salt, $^1/_2$ teaspoon freshly ground pepper, and oregano.

2   Lay cheese over turkey, leaving $^1/_2$ inch around edges. Fold cheese where necessary. Place a sun-dried tomato at narrowest end of each cutlet. Then starting from tomato end, roll up snugly, to form a cylinder. Moisten outsides with 1 tablespoon reserved tomato oil. Secure with toothpicks.

3 Grill turkey roulades, turning to cook all sides, until golden brown and just cooked through, about 15 minutes. Remove toothpicks and serve hot.

4 SERVINGS

SIMPLE TIP *If the cutlets are unevenly thick, lightly pound the thick parts with a meat mallet or the bottom of your fist until they're even.*

SERVING SUGGESTIONS *Steamed greens such as spinach or chard or Balsamic Caesar Salad (page 172). Good with grilled potatoes.*

VARIATION *Sprinkle the cutlets with garlic powder before covering with the cheese.*

Turkey and Snow Pea Stir-Fry

In this simple stir-fry, tender strips of white turkey and crunchy pea pods are tossed in a rich, brown sauce sparked by vinegar and pepper. The cooking is done in the blink of an eye, so be sure to have all the ingredients prepped and ready by the stove.

$1/2$ pound snow peas
1 pound turkey breast cutlets
2 tablespoons soy sauce
1 tablespoon red wine vinegar
$1^3/_4$ teaspoons cornstarch
3 tablespoons vegetable oil

1   String snow peas. Rinse cutlets and dry with paper towels. Cut against grain into $1/8$-inch-thick strips. In a small bowl, mix soy sauce with vinegar, cornstarch, 3 tablespoons water, and $1/2$ teaspoon each salt and pepper. Set sauce aside.

2   Heat 1 tablespoon oil in a wok or very large skillet over high heat. Add snow peas and cook, stirring and tossing constantly, until the color brightens, about

1 minute. Transfer to a platter. Add remaining oil to wok and when almost smoking, add turkey. Cook, stirring, tossing, and separating strips with a spatula, until they look mostly white, about 1 minute.

3   Return snow peas to wok with turkey. Reduce heat to medium. Give sauce a stir and add to wok. Bring to boil, stirring. Cook until sauce thickens and turns clear, 1 minute. Serve hot.

3 TO 4 SERVINGS

SERVING SUGGESTIONS *Stir-fried eggplant or red cabbage. Steamed rice. Or serve over fresh Chinese noodles or angel hair pasta first boiled, then sautéed into a flat, crisp brown cake.*

VARIATION *Add more crunch to the dish with sliced, canned water chestnuts. Or give it an earthy note with a few thinly sliced fresh shiitake mushroom caps cooked with the snow peas.*

Tender

Meats

Grilled Ginger Steak

Often a grilled steak is great just on its own. But sometimes it's nice to add another accent to bring out the beefy flavor even more. Here, mustard, soy sauce, and fresh ginger do the trick.

2 boneless New York strip steaks, 1 pound each, cut 1 to 1¼ inches thick
1 large garlic clove, cut in half lengthwise
2 teaspoons soy sauce
2 teaspoons Dijon mustard
1 tablespoon vegetable oil
2 teaspoons grated fresh ginger

1 Prepare a medium-hot fire in a barbecue grill. Dry steaks with paper towels. Rub both sides well with cut garlic. Stir together soy sauce, mustard, and oil in a small bowl until mixed. Spread over both sides of steaks.

2 Grill first side of steaks until well browned, about 3 minutes. Turn over and cook 2 minutes more, until browned. Move to cooler part of grill, cover, and cook until medium-rare, 3 to 5 minutes.

3   Transfer to a platter and season with salt and pepper to taste. Spread ginger over top of meat, then let rest 3 minutes. Slice thinly across the grain and serve with the juices.

4 SERVINGS

SIMPLE TIP *Grated ginger is stronger than chopped because more of the pungent juice is released. After peeling the ginger, grate the piece on the medium perforations of a box grater. Use only the soft and juicy parts that come through the grater. Bits clinging to the outside gratings are fibrous and tough.*

SERVING SUGGESTIONS *Sugar snap peas or Mushrooms with Bacon and Scallions (page 138). Baked potatoes or Rustic Onion Rolls (page 152).*

Grilled Steak Fajitas with Ancho Chile Salsa

Here's the fajita story. Part one: Rosy slices of steak are stuffed into warm tortillas. Part two: The steak is doused in an earthy, not-too-hot Mexican salsa. Part three: A rich avocado mash garnishes all and ends the tale. Skirt steak, the type called for here, is a beefy-tasting cut with deep, satisfying flavor. But flank, sirloin, rib, or London broil would be just fine, too.

2 dried ancho chilies
1 medium tomato
1 small red onion
2 avocados
8 flour tortillas, 6 to 7 inches in diameter
1^1/$_2$ pounds skirt steak
2 teaspoons vegetable oil

1 Prepare a hot fire in a barbecue grill. Slit open one side of each chile. Reserve ^{1}/$_4$ teaspoon of seeds. Discard rest along with stems. Soak chiles in hot water to cover until pliable, about 15 minutes. Cut tomato into ^{1}/$_2$-inch dice. Cut enough onion into small dice to measure ^{1}/$_4$ cup.

2 Puree chiles with ^{1}/$_4$ cup soaking water in a blender or food processor until

almost smooth, about 2 minutes. Add a little more water, if necessary. Transfer 3 tablespoons chile puree to a small bowl; save or freeze any if left. Stir in tomato, onion, and chile seeds. Season with salt. Cut avocados in half and discard pits. Scoop out pulp and mash in a bowl with a fork. Season with salt and pepper to taste.

3 Grill both sides of tortillas to heat through. Stack, wrap in foil, and keep warm. Season steaks generously with salt and pepper. Rub with oil. Grill first side until brown, about 3 minutes. Turn over and cook until medium-rare, 3 to 4 minutes more. Thinly slice steaks across grain. Serve right away with tortillas, avocado, and salsa on the side.

4 SERVINGS

SIMPLE TIP *It's the seeds and stems that contain most of the chile's heat. If you'd like to turn up this salsa's temperature, simply add more seeds.*

SERVING SUGGESTIONS *Grilled corn on the cob and grilled fresh poblano chiles cut into strips, which can be added to the fajitas, or Corn in Parmesan Garlic Cream (page 130). In cool weather, start with Black Bean and Bacon Soup (page 4).*

VARIATION *Grill individual steaks and serve them topped with this fresh salsa, or a jarred one and the avocado. Serve the tortillas as a bread on the side. Instead of grilling each tortilla, heat a foil-wrapped stack of them.*

Oven-Roasted Steak with Herbed Salt and Pepper

Sometimes there's nothing more desirable than a big, fat juicy steak. This one is seasoned with lots of salt and pepper, fennel, and rosemary before roasting and then again after. It's a straightforward touch that emphasizes the meat's beefiness in the simplest possible way. As far as cooking goes, the steak is first seared in a skillet on top of the stove, then finished in the oven. And if you wonder where to buy such luxurious steak without spending a fortune, look for it at your local discount club.

1 teaspoon ground fennel seed
1 teaspoon dried rosemary
2 pounds T-bone steak, cut 2 inches thick
1 tablespoon olive oil
1 tablespoon butter

1   Preheat the oven to 350°F. Mix fennel and rosemary in a small bowl with $1\frac{1}{2}$ teaspoons coarse salt and 1 teaspoon freshly ground pepper. Dry steak with paper towels. Sprinkle half of herbed salt over both sides, pressing it in.

2 Heat olive oil in a large, heavy ovenproof skillet, preferably cast-iron, over high heat. Add steak and brown first side until crusted, 3 to 5 minutes. Turn over and brown 2 minutes. Transfer skillet to oven and cook until medium-rare, about 15 minutes.

3 Remove steak to a cutting board and let rest 8 minutes. Pour off fat and reserve skillet. Cut steak from bone, slice thinly across the grain, and lay overlapping on a platter. Melt butter in skillet and pour over steak. Sprinkle with remaining herbed salt and serve right away.

4 SERVINGS

SIMPLE TIP *A heavy skillet is important for getting a good crust on the steak. I'm a big fan of cast-iron but others, such as Calphalon or those made of heavy-gauge aluminum, work well, too.*

SERVING SUGGESTIONS *Sautéed Red Cabbage with Parmesan Cheese (page 134) or Lemon-Caper Carrots (page 128). Roasted potatoes or Smashed Potatoes with Fresh Basil (page 158).*

VARIATION *Substitute a teaspoon or so of dried tarragon or anise seed for the fennel. Use a boneless rib-eye instead of a T-bone.*

Salt and Pepper Burgers

I'm a burger lover, and I don't like them too messed with. The likes of cheese and bacon or sautéed onions will do me fine. But here's another take that's fun to eat and doesn't stray too far from the basics. It's a cracked pepper burger, which is cooked in a searingly hot salted skillet. The peppercorns add spiciness and a little texture. Oh, yes, there's a quick bit of sauce at the end for ratcheting up the taste even more.

2 teaspoons whole black peppercorns

$1^3/_4$ pounds ground beef or chuck

4 kaiser rolls

2 tablespoons butter

1 tablespoon Worcestershire sauce

2 teaspoons Dijon mustard

1   Place peppercorns on a kitchen towel and fold to cover. Crack with a meat mallet or back of a small skillet. Form beef into 4 burgers 1 inch thick. Sprinkle one side of each with peppercorns and press in lightly.

2   Split and toast rolls; keep warm. Sprinkle 1 teaspoon kosher salt over bottom

of a large, heavy skillet over high heat. When hot, add burgers peppered side down and cook until crusted on the bottom, about 3 minutes. Turn over and cook 3 minutes more for medium-rare. Remove from heat.

3 Set burgers on roll bottoms. Melt butter in still hot skillet and stir in Worcestershire sauce and mustard. Spoon half of sauce over burgers and rest over cut side of tops. Cover burgers with tops and serve.

4 SERVINGS

SIMPLE TIPS *Place the peppercorns in a zipper type bag instead of in a folded towel. Zip up the bag and pound the peppercorns.*

A searingly hot salted skillet and high heat allow the meat to crust beautifully.

SERVING SUGGESTIONS *Lemon Coleslaw (page 180) or Mushrooms with Bacon and Scallions (page 138). Baked potatoes drizzled with olive oil and sprinkled with chopped sun-dried tomatoes or Roasted Baked Potatoes (page 160).*

Smothered Mini-Meat Loaves

If you imagine individual meat loaves blanketed by a rich tomato and onion–thick sauce, you've got the picture. These babies are different from big meat loaf in a couple of other ways, too. First, they're mixed with sour cream instead of the traditional milk-soaked crumbs. Then they're cooked on top of the stove from start to finish. No need to fire up the oven.

1³/₄ pounds ground beef
¹/₂ cup sour cream
1 tablespoon olive oil
1 medium-large onion, chopped
2 large garlic cloves, chopped
¹/₂ cup canned crushed tomatoes in puree

1   In a large bowl, combine ground beef, sour cream, 1 teaspoon salt, and ¹/₂ teaspoon freshly ground pepper. Divide into 4 portions. Pat into slightly flattened, football-shaped loaves about 5 inches long and 1 inch thick.

2   Heat olive oil in a large skillet over high heat. Lightly brown loaves on one side, about 2 minutes. Carefully turn over and brown other side, about 2 min-

utes. Transfer meat loaves to a platter. Pour off all but 1 tablespoon from skillet. Reduce heat to low and add onion. Cook, stirring occasionally, until lightly browned and tender, 3 minutes. Stir in garlic and cook 30 seconds.

3 Return meat loaves to skillet and distribute onion around. Add tomatoes and $1/4$ cup water. Stir around loaves to combine sauce as best as possible. Cover and cook over low heat, turning once, 7 to 8 minutes. Set loaves on plates. Season sauce with salt and pepper. Pour over loaves and serve hot.

4 SERVINGS

SIMPLE TIP *If the sauce is watery when the loaves are done, boil it down for a minute or two until it's thick and rich. Then pour it over the loaves.*

SERVING SUGGESTIONS *Spinach salad with cucumber and radishes or Green Beans with Nutmeg and Lemon (page 135). Buttered dried or fresh egg noodles or Garden Mashed Potatoes (page 156).*

VARIATION *Add $1/2$ teaspoon dried thyme or oregano to the sauce. If you like, use a packaged mixture of beef, veal, and pork instead of all beef.*

Curried Lamb Chops

What a boon to find thick, meaty lamb chops at the discount club. I've always been a lamb chop lover and now buying them doesn't have to be such an indulgence. If you feel that way, too, then try these chops. They're dredged in flour and curry powder. Then they're cooked until the outsides turn brown and crisp and the insides a luscious, juicy pink.

2 tablespoons flour
1 tablespoon curry powder
4 loin lamb chops, 7 ounces each, cut 1$\frac{1}{2}$ to 2 inches thick
1 tablespoon fresh lemon juice
1 tablespoon vegetable oil

1   Preheat oven to 350°F. Mix flour with curry powder. Season with $\frac{1}{4}$ teaspoon salt and $\frac{1}{4}$ teaspoon freshly ground pepper. Dip both sides of chops into lemon juice. Then dredge well in seasoned flour.

2   Heat oil in a large, ovenproof skillet over medium-high heat. Add chops and cook first side until golden brown, 2 to 3 minutes. Turn over and lightly brown second side, 1 to 2 minutes. Pour off fat from pan.

3 Transfer to oven and roast, turning once, until medium-rare, 8 to 10 minutes. Serve hot.

4 SERVINGS

SIMPLE TIP *If you like your chops browned all around, then brown all the edges before putting them into the oven.*

SERVING SUGGESTIONS *Slow-Sautéed Turnips (page 143) and/or mango chutney. Plain couscous or Tomato Couscous (page 168).*

VARIATION *Not a curry fan? Then try brushing both sides of the chops with a mixture of mustard and lemon juice before dredging in flour.*

Grilled Rosemary and Garlic Lamb Burgers

Here's a lamb burger that's quickly seasoned, then grilled until juicy-pink. And in case you're wondering, the garlic, rosemary, and soy sauce spicing adds interest without masking the naturally distinctive flavor of the meat.

1³⁄₄ pounds ground lamb
1 large garlic clove, minced
1 teaspoon dried rosemary
1¹⁄₂ tablespoons soy sauce

1   Prepare a medium-hot fire in a barbecue grill.

2   With a fork, mix ground lamb in a large bowl with garlic, rosemary, and ¹⁄₂ teaspoon freshly ground pepper. Form into 4 burgers, 1 inch thick.

3   Grill, turning once, until deeply browned on both sides and pink inside, about 10 minutes. Serve hot.

4 SERVINGS

SIMPLE TIP *The burgers turn out well, too, when cooked in a heavy skillet with a few drops of oil over high heat.*

SERVING SUGGESTIONS *Sugar snap peas or Carrot and Apple Salad with Tahini Dressing (page 174). Warm Italian bread or Savory Noodle Pie (page 166).*

DRESS IT UP *Top the burgers with a dollop of mayonnaise that's been seasoned with chopped fresh tarragon or basil and more garlic.*

BBQ Pork

This dish is a little like a stew with its chunks of meat and lots of sauce. But unlike a stew, this one cooks in merely a few minutes, since the meat is cut from tender chops. Strips of green pepper are part of it, too, stir-fried first then added back at the end. That way their freshness contrasts with the rich barbecue flavor of the sauce.

1 large green bell pepper

1^1/$_2$ pounds boneless pork chops, about 1 inch thick

^{1}/$_4$ cup olive oil

4 teaspoons flour

^{3}/$_4$ cup barbecue sauce

1^1/$_4$ teaspoons dried oregano

1   Cut pepper in half and discard stem, seeds, and whitish membranes. Cut into thin strips. Trim fat off chops. Cut into 1^1/$_2$- to 2-inch pieces. Dry with paper towels.

2   Heat 1^1/$_2$ tablespoons of olive oil in a large, deep skillet or Dutch oven over medium heat. Stir-fry peppers until very crisp, about 2 minutes. Transfer to

plate. Add remaining 2 1/2 tablespoons oil and increase heat to medium-high. Working in 2 batches, brown pork. Sprinkle over flour and cook, stirring, 30 seconds. Stir in barbecue sauce and 2/3 cup water.

3   Bring to a boil, stirring. Reduce heat to low and simmer, covered, until pork is almost cooked through, about 2 minutes. Stir in oregano and pepper strips and cook 1 to 2 minutes more. Season with salt and pepper to taste. Serve hot.

4 SERVINGS

SERVING SUGGESTIONS *Roast Tomatoes Provençal (page 140) or Corn in Parmesan Garlic Cream (page 130). Plain boiled rice or steamed potatoes for soaking up the sauce.*

DRESS IT UP *Make the dish with a mixture of chicken, fresh pork, and a smoked pork chop cut into chunks. Using half of a red and half of a green bell pepper will add extra color.*

VARIATION *Make this with chunks of chicken breast or boneless thighs cut into pieces instead of pork. The thighs would have to cook for longer, of course.*

Mozzarella Pork Burgers in Garlic Bread

There's a surprising amount of chili powder in these pork burgers. Surprising because what it does to the meat is season it well, not make it taste like chili. When the burgers are served, they're covered in melted mozzarella and sandwiched in garlic bread. Dare I say it? I think these big guys belong in the company of a classic hamburger.

2 medium-large garlic cloves, minced
3 tablespoons olive oil
$1/2$ large loaf Italian bread
$1^3/_4$ pounds ground pork
2 tablespoons chili powder
4 slices mozzarella cheese, each about $1/4$ inch thick

1 Mix garlic with 2 tablespoons olive oil in a small bowl. Cut bread into four 3-inch sections. Split horizontally and turn cut sides up. Spread garlic oil over bread using the back of a spoon. Toast under a broiler and keep warm.

2   In a large bowl, sprinkle pork with chili powder, $^3/_4$ teaspoon salt, and $^1/_2$ teaspoon freshly ground pepper. Combine with a fork. Form into 4 burgers, $^3/_4$ inch thick.

3   Heat remaining 1 tablespoon oil in a large skillet over medium-high heat. Add burgers and brown bottoms until crusted, 3 minutes. Turn over and reduce heat to low. Lay cheese on burgers, cover skillet, and cook 4 minutes more. Set burgers on bread bottoms and drizzle with pan juices. Cover with tops and serve.

4 SERVINGS

SIMPLE TIP *Naturally, the hotter the chili powder, the more kick it adds.*

SERVING SUGGESTIONS *Pickles, olives, and cherry tomatoes or Lemon Coleslaw (page 180). Potato or vegetable chips or potato salad.*

VARIATION *Lay a slice of ripe tomato or big piece of roasted pepper on top of the cheese.*

Grill-Roasted Italian Sausages with Potatoes and Mushrooms

This is a fun one to make. First, sausages are browned over glowing coals. Then they're placed on top of mushrooms and potatoes lying on foil rectangles. The foil edges are crimped together to make packets that can cook in the heat of a covered grill without any juices escaping. I like to serve them just as they are: hot silver pouches plopped onto plates. All you have to do is open the tops, let the savory steam waft out, and dive in with your fork and knife.

10 ounces white button mushrooms
4 medium boiling potatoes
8 links sweet Italian sausage with fennel, $1^1/_2$ pounds total
$1^1/_2$ tablespoons olive oil

1   Prepare a medium-hot fire in a barbecue grill. Quarter mushrooms. Scrub potatoes, then slice $^1/_4$ inch thick. Prick sausages several times with a fork.

2 Cut 4 pieces of 12-inch-wide foil into 28-inch lengths. Fold lengthwise to make 12 by 14-inch rectangles. Place mushrooms and potatoes in a large bowl. Toss with olive oil. Toss again with $1/2$ teaspoon salt and $1/2$ teaspoon freshly ground pepper. Spread over center of each foil rectangle.

3 Set sausages on grill. Cook, turning, until all sides are golden brown, 4 to 5 minutes. Set 2 sausages on each serving of mushrooms and potatoes. Bring up foil sides to meet. Fold about 1 inch from each side together to seal tightly. Place packets on rack and cover grill. Cook 20 minutes. Set on plates, carefully unfold to partially open tops, and serve hot.

4 SERVINGS

SERVING SUGGESTIONS *Watercress and Belgian endive salad, sliced tomatoes vinaigrette, or Balsamic Caesar Salad (page 172) with radishes.*

VARIATIONS *Substitute any other large link sausage made of chicken, turkey, veal, or pork, spicy or not.*

Add a few chunky pieces of summer squash to each packet.

Pork Chops with Jalapeño Tomato Sauce

Yes, this sauce is fiery. And it's the seeds of the jalapeño that make most of the heat. Of course, you can tone down the heat by deseeding the chile first, if you'd rather.

1 small to medium jalapeño pepper

1 small onion

4 boneless center-cut pork chops, 7 ounces each, cut 1 inch thick

1^1⁄$_2$ tablespoons vegetable oil

1 garlic clove, chopped

1 cup canned crushed tomatoes in puree

1   Thinly slice jalapeño, seeds and all, into thin rounds. Finely chop onion. Dry the pork chops with paper towels. Season with salt and pepper.

2   Heat oil in a large skillet over medium-high heat. Brown fat edge of chops, about 2 minutes. Then lightly brown both sides, about 3 minutes total. Transfer to a plate.

3   Reduce heat to medium-low and add onion, jalapeño, and garlic to the skillet. Brown lightly, stirring, 2 to 3 minutes. Stir in tomatoes and season with salt

to taste. Lay chops over sauce. Cover and cook until just cooked through, about 5 minutes. Serve pork chops topped with sauce.

4 SERVINGS

SIMPLE TIP *I used an average-size jalapeño for this recipe. However, it's good to know that 2 jalapeños of the same size can differ in heat levels. So if the sauce doesn't set your mouth on fire, your jalapeño was probably a less incendiary one. Add more heat, if you like, with dashes of hot sauce.*

SERVING SUGGESTIONS *A plate of sliced avocados with lime wedges for squeezing, sautéed zucchini, or Corn in Parmesan Garlic Cream (page 130). A stack of steaming tortillas or Silver Dollar Corn Cakes (page 148).*

Cuban Pork Chops

In Cuba, lots of garlic, freshly squeezed lime juice, and aromatic cumin are a favorite way to season roast pork. I think the combo is good with chops, too. Here, meaty chops cook on top of the stove while their lime and garlic pan juices reduce to a syrupy sauce around them.

4 large garlic cloves

4 center-cut pork chops, 8 ounces each, cut 1 inch thick

1$\frac{1}{2}$ tablespoons olive oil

$\frac{1}{3}$ cup fresh lime juice

$\frac{3}{4}$ teaspoon ground cumin

1   Thinly slice garlic. Dry pork chops with paper towels. Season generously with salt.

2   Heat olive oil in a large skillet over medium heat. Stand and brown fat edge of chops, about 2 minutes. Brown first side, about 2 minutes. Turn over, and brown 1 minute more. Scatter garlic around chops and cook, stirring, 15 seconds. Add lime juice and $\frac{1}{4}$ cup water.

3 Cook, uncovered, turning chops once or twice, until done and $1/4$ cup syrupy juices remain, 6 to 8 minutes. Transfer chops to plates and spoon sauce on top. Sprinkle with cumin and season with freshly ground pepper. Serve hot.

4 SERVINGS

SIMPLE TIP *If the pan juices reduce too much before the chops are done, add a little more water. If you add too much, just boil down the juices after the chops are out of the pan.*
SERVING SUGGESTIONS *Spinach or Swiss chard or cooked carrots sautéed with red bell peppers. Plain buttered rice or rice mixed with black beans.*

Vegetable

Side Dishes

Roasted Asparagus with Parmesan Crumbs

Roasting asparagus is a simple technique. It requires nothing more than the fresh spears, olive oil, salt, pepper, and a hot oven. However, I like to do just a little more: sprinkle them with bread crumbs and grated Parmesan cheese toward the end of roasting. The cheese and crumbs turn golden and toasty and add a bit of rustic character.

1 pound medium asparagus spears
3 tablespoons olive oil
1 tablespoon plain dry bread crumbs
1 tablespoon freshly grated Parmesan cheese

1   Preheat oven to 425°F. Snap off tough ends of asparagus. About 5 minutes before cooking, heat a roasting pan in oven with olive oil. Mix bread crumbs and cheese in a small bowl.

2   Add asparagus to pan and roll to coat with oil. Roast until when one is lifted in the middle with tongs, the ends bend slightly, 10 to 12 minutes.

3   Sprinkle with crumbs and cheese, and roast until golden, 3 to 5 minutes. Season with salt and freshly ground pepper. Serve asparagus hot, topped with any crumbs and cheese left in pan.

4 SERVINGS

SIMPLE TIP *Choose a roasting pan that's large enough to hold the asparagus in a single layer; otherwise they will steam rather than roast.*

Stir-Fried Broccoli with Garlic

Stir-frying is the perfect way to cook broccoli if you like yours bright green and crunchy. In this version, the technique is Chinese, but the cooking oil is olive, and it works just fine.

1 large bunch broccoli
3 tablespoons olive oil
1 large garlic clove, minced

1   Trim large stems of broccoli. Cut heads into 2-inch florets.

2   Heat olive oil in a wok or very large skillet over medium heat. When hot, add broccoli. Cook, stirring and tossing, until color deepens, about 2 minutes. Stir in garlic, then immediately add $1/4$ cup water.

3   Toss and stir until water is gone and garlic *just* starts to color, 1 to 2 minutes. Remove from heat and season with salt and freshly ground pepper. Serve hot, warm, or at room temperature.

4 SERVINGS

SIMPLE TIP *If you use a smaller skillet, the water may not evaporate by the time the broccoli is done. If that happens, remove the broccoli with a slotted spoon and let the water boil away. Then toss the broccoli back in for a few seconds to mingle with the garlic.*

VARIATION *Peel the stems with a paring knife to their tender core. Slice them thinly on the diagonal and stir-fry along with the florets.*

Lemon-Caper Carrots

You might call these carrots "sweet and sour," but that wouldn't do them justice unless you added the word *refined.* Their sweetness is discreet, the lemon light and refreshing, and the capers a briny highlight. These are good at room temperature, chilled, or right out of the pan, so make them at any time.

1 pound carrots
1 1/2 tablespoons fresh lemon juice
1 tablespoon sugar
3 tablespoons olive oil
1 tablespoon nonpareil capers

1 Bring a large saucepan of salted water to a boil over medium-high heat. Cut the carrots on a diagonal into 1/4-inch-thick slices. Cook until firm-tender, about 5 minutes. Drain carrots and set pan over low heat for a few seconds to dry.

2 Add lemon juice, sugar, olive oil, and capers. Cook briefly, stirring, to dissolve sugar. Add carrots.

3 Cook, stirring occasionally, until carrots are fully tender, about 2 minutes. Season with salt and freshly ground pepper to taste. Serve hot, at room temperature, or chilled.

4 SERVINGS

SIMPLE TIP *Don't race out to buy the small nonpareil capers if you have large ones. Just chop what you've got, then measure them.*

Corn in Parmesan Garlic Cream

The name pretty much says it all: sweet corn kernels bathed in a delicate cream sauce seasoned with garlic and grated Parmesan cheese. Reggiano from Italy, of course, is the best. So is grating it right before you use it.

1 box (10 ounces) frozen corn
1 tablespoon butter
1 large garlic clove, minced
$1/2$ cup heavy cream
3 tablespoons freshly grated Parmesan cheese

1   Bring a large pot of water to a boil over high heat. Add corn, stir once, then drain.

2   Melt butter in a medium skillet over low heat. Add garlic and cook, stirring, 30 seconds. Add cream and boil until lightly thickened, stirring occasionally, about 2 minutes.

3 Stir in corn and heat through, 30 to 60 seconds. Remove from heat and stir in cheese. Season with salt and freshly ground pepper to taste. Serve hot.

3 TO 4 SERVINGS

SIMPLE TIP *A 10-ounce box of corn measures 2 cups. That's handy to know in case you buy your corn in a large bag and not a box.*

Sesame Edamame

As my husband says, "Where have these been all my life?" An Asian staple, edamame are fresh green soybeans, which taste something like a lima bean crossed with a pea. Now they've made their way into the frozen food section of the market. In this recipe, they're cooked with soy sauce and tossed with toasted sesame seeds.

2 teaspoons sesame seeds
1 tablespoon soy sauce
1/2 pound frozen shelled soybeans (edamame)
1 teaspoon Asian sesame oil

1   Toast sesame seeds in a small skillet over low heat, shaking pan, until light gold, 1 to 2 minutes.

2   Bring 1/2 cup water and soy sauce to a boil in a large saucepan over medium-high heat. Add edamame and cook, covered, until tender, 5 minutes. Uncover and boil away any liquid, if necessary, 1 to 2 minutes.

3 Remove from heat. Season with salt, then stir in sesame oil and toasted sesame seeds. Serve hot.

3 TO 4 SERVINGS

SIMPLE TIP *If you buy edamame in large bags, $1/2$ pound measures about $1^2/_3$ cups.*

VARIATION *For a spicy version, stir in drops of hot Szechuan oil to taste with the sesame oil.*

Sautéed Red Cabbage with Parmesan Cheese

Red cabbage turns sweet and tender when you sauté it. Simple enough, for sure. But you can go one tiny step farther by stirring in a smidgen of grated cheese. Just a little bit will deepen the flavor without giving away the secret. It makes a fine match for chicken, turkey, and pork.

1 small head red cabbage
2 tablespoons butter
1 1/2 tablespoons freshly grated Parmesan cheese

1 Cut cabbage in half and core. Thinly slice enough to measure 6 cups.

2 Melt butter in a large skillet over medium heat. Add cabbage and season with salt and freshly ground pepper. Cook, stirring occasionally, until wilted but slightly crisp, about 5 minutes.

3 Stir in cheese and serve hot.

4 SERVINGS

Green Beans with Nutmeg and Lemon

Everybody likes green beans, even people who don't usually eat vegetables. And they're so popular, you really don't have to do much to make them welcome. That said, here's one of my favorite ways to serve beans.

1¼ pounds green beans, trimmed
1½ tablespoons butter
½ teaspoon grated nutmeg
1½ teaspoons fresh lemon juice

1 Bring a large pot of salted water to a boil over high heat. Add green beans, return to a boil, and cook until tender-crisp, 4 to 5 minutes. Drain beans well.

2 Melt butter in a large skillet over medium heat. Add beans and toss in butter. Cook, stirring occasionally, 2 minutes.

3 Sprinkle with nutmeg. Season with salt and freshly ground pepper. Stir in lemon juice and serve hot.

4 SERVINGS

Wilted Green Beans with Red Onion

These green beans drink in the rich flavor of olive oil and sweet onion during their slow cooking. They become soft and tender while the onion practically melts around them. Then a splash of vinegar provides a little lift. Don't expect the finished dish to be all pretty and bright green, though. The color is dulled. But the flavor isn't.

1 $1/4$ pounds green beans, trimmed
1 medium-to-large red onion, thinly sliced
3 tablespoons olive oil
2 teaspoons red wine vinegar

1   Rinse beans and drain well.

2   Place beans and onion in a large saucepan over high heat. Drizzle with olive oil, season with salt to taste, and stir together. When sizzling starts, reduce heat to low and cover.

3 Cook, stirring occasionally, until beans are very tender, 25 to 30 minutes. If liquid remains, uncover and cook, stirring, until gone, 1 to 2 minutes. Stir in the vinegar and season with freshly ground pepper to taste.

4 SERVINGS

SIMPLE TIP *These beans can be served hot, warm, or at room temperature. You can even serve them as a salad if you add a little extra vinegar at the end.*

VARIATION *Add ½ cup of drained, chopped canned tomatoes to the raw beans and onion.*

Mushrooms with Bacon and Scallions

These savory mushrooms are meant to accompany the likes of steak, burgers, chicken, and chops. But they're also good tossed with pasta (and more olive oil) for dinner. Or spooned into the middle of a steaming baked potato for a light supper or lunch.

1 pound mushrooms
4 strips bacon
3 scallions
1$^1/_2$ teaspoons olive oil
$^1/_2$ teaspoon dried thyme

1   Quarter mushrooms or cut into eighths, if large. Cut bacon into $^1/_4$-inch-wide strips. Cut white part of scallions into $^1/_2$-inch-long pieces. Thinly slice green part of 1 scallion.

2   Heat olive oil in a large skillet over medium heat. Add bacon and cook, stirring, just until fat renders, about 2 minutes. Add mushrooms and white of scallions. Cook, stirring occasionally, until water evaporates and mushrooms and bacon begin to brown, about 10 minutes.

3   Season with thyme, salt, and freshly ground pepper. Stir in scallion green and serve hot.

4 SERVINGS

SIMPLE TIP *Some bacon is less fatty than others. If your batch of cooked mushrooms seems a little dry, stir in another teaspoon or so of olive oil at the end.*

DRESS IT UP *Add a little heavy cream after the mushroom juices evaporate and cook for a minute or so until the cream thickens slightly. Then stir in the scallion green.*

Roast Tomatoes Provençal

You know how a leg of lamb is often studded with slivers of garlic before roasting? Well, that's what goes on with these tomatoes under their topping of thyme-flavored bread crumbs. The tomatoes to choose, by the way, are ones fully ripe but still firm so they won't collapse in the oven. And, of course, the better the tomato, the better the taste.

2 large tomatoes, ripe but firm
2 medium garlic cloves, slivered lengthwise
$1/4$ cup plain dry bread crumbs
3 tablespoons extra-virgin olive oil
$3/4$ teaspoon dried thyme

1 Preheat oven to 450°F with the rack at the top. Cut tomatoes in half horizontally. Cut a thin slice off bottoms so they sit flat. Insert slivers of garlic into tops of tomatoes, making small cuts first where necessary. Season lightly with salt and freshly ground pepper.

2   Place bread crumbs in a small bowl and stir in 1¹⁄₂ tablespoons of olive oil. Season with thyme, salt, and freshly ground pepper to taste. Pat mixture over tops of tomatoes.

3   Grease a small baking pan with remaining oil. Set tomatoes in pan. Roast until sides feel soft when lightly pressed and crumbs have browned, 15 to 18 minutes. Serve hot or warm, drizzled with any oil in pan.

4 SERVINGS

SIMPLE TIP *If the tomatoes collapse, don't worry. Cut them into quarters, then scoop them up and serve them in a bowl. Call them savory garlic tomatoes.*

VARIATION *Prepare tomatoes and roast until they almost collapse. Chop them coarsely and toss with pasta, all their juices, and more olive oil.*

Sautéed Grape Tomatoes, Chicago Style

I grew up in Chicago, where hot dogs are king. On the North Side where I lived, a good dog had juicy wedges of tomato tucked alongside in the bun, with celery salt sprinkled over all. I loved the combo then, and I still do. But now, I'm just as likely to go for the tomatoes alone tossed in sizzling butter with their deliciously salty celery enhancement.

1 $1/2$ tablespoons butter
1 pint grape tomatoes
1 teaspoon celery salt

1 Melt butter in a large skillet over medium heat. Add tomatoes. Cook, rolling them in the pan, until wrinkled but still round and intact, about 3 minutes.

2 Transfer tomatoes and buttery pan juices to a bowl. Sprinkle with celery salt, toss gently, and serve.

4 SERVINGS

VARIATION *Use cherry tomatoes in place of the grape tomatoes.*

Slow-Sautéed Turnips

I love to cook turnips, oh-so-slowly, in a pan on top of the stove. Their natural sugars are drawn out in the gently sizzling olive oil, and they turn tender and golden brown at the same time.

1¹⁄₄ pounds medium white turnips
2¹⁄₂ tablespoons olive oil

1   Peel turnips and cut in half lengthwise. Lay cut sides down and slice ¹⁄₂ inch thick.

2   Heat olive oil in a large skillet over medium-low heat. Add turnips and stir to coat with oil. Season with salt.

3   Cook, stirring occasionally, until turnips are golden brown and tender, 15 to 20 minutes. Season lightly with pepper and serve.

4 SERVINGS

SIMPLE TIP *A fresh turnip has a smooth, creamy white and purple skin. When squeezed, it should feel hard and dense.*

Grilled Zucchini with Balsamic Dressing

Let's face it, zucchini is not an exciting vegetable. But it can be very good if cooked and seasoned in a lively fashion. Grilling, for instance, injects a smoky quality, and the light charring highlights its juicy nature. Then when you add a potent dressing made from mustard, soy sauce, and balsamic vinegar, the simple squash really gets a blast of flavor.

1 teaspoon Dijon mustard
2 tablespoons balsamic vinegar
2 teaspoons soy sauce
4 medium zucchini
3 tablespoons olive oil

1   Prepare a medium fire in a barbecue grill. Place mustard in a small bowl and whisk in balsamic vinegar and soy sauce. Season with salt and freshly ground pepper. Set dressing aside.

2   Scrub and dry zucchini. Trim ends and cut in half lengthwise. Toss zucchini with olive oil in a large bowl to coat. Transfer zucchini cut sides down to rack;

reserve bowl with leftover oil. Grill until browned on bottom. Turn and cook until firm-tender, about 10 minutes total.

3   Remove zucchini from grill and cut diagonally into 1-inch pieces. Return to bowl with oil. Add dressing and toss. Serve hot, at room temperature, or chilled.

4 SERVINGS

SIMPLE TIP *You can tell if the zucchini are cooked just enough without cutting into it. With tongs, pick up one in the middle and if its 2 ends bend slightly, it's done.*

VARIATION *If you like lighter flavor, use fresh lemon juice instead of vinegar. But use less of it since it's sharper. Either way, a bit of minced garlic is a good addition, too.*

Comforting

Carbs

Silver Dollar Corn Cakes

These little cakes have lots of corn bread taste. And they cook in about two minutes in the pan. I like them best when they're made with butter, but vegetable oil can be substituted, if you'd rather. Either way, don't crowd them as they cook. Four at a time will fit comfortably in a nine-inch skillet and can stay warm in a low oven while you finish the rest.

1 cup yellow cornmeal
$^1/_2$ teaspoon baking soda
1 large egg
$^1/_2$ cup buttermilk
1$^1/_2$ tablespoons light brown sugar
3 tablespoons butter, melted

1   Combine cornmeal, baking soda, $^1/_4$ teaspoon salt, and 2 grinds pepper in a large bowl. Lightly beat egg in a small bowl. Then stir in buttermilk, brown sugar, and 1 tablespoon melted butter. Pour into dry ingredients and stir until smooth.

2   Heat a griddle or large skillet over low heat. Brush with butter. When hot, drop batter 1 tablespoon at a time, spreading each cake slightly with back of a spoon. Cook until golden brown, about 1 minute. Turn over and cook until each cake is puffed and underside is golden, about 1 minute.

3   Continue making cakes, brushing griddle with butter between each batch, until all batter is used. Serve hot.

4 SERVINGS, 12 2$\frac{1}{2}$-INCH CAKES

VARIATION *Add 2 tablespoons thinly sliced scallions to the batter.*

Savory Cheddar Cheese Muffins

You wouldn't think something as packed with cheese as these muffins would be feather light. But they are. Some of that is due to the olive oil in the batter, which performs a little magic. Not only does it help give them good texture, but also it coaxes out maximum flavor from the ingredients without letting on that it's in there.

1 cup plus 2 tablespoons all-purpose flour

2 teaspoons baking powder

1 large egg

$1/4$ cup olive oil

$1/2$ cup milk

$3/4$ teaspoon dried dill

1 cup shredded extra-sharp Cheddar cheese

1 Preheat oven to 450°F. Combine flour and baking powder with $1/4$ teaspoon salt and 1 grind of pepper in a large bowl. Lightly beat egg in a medium bowl, then stir in olive oil, milk, and dill. Blend in cheese.

2   Pour liquid into dry ingredients. Mix with a fork until just combined. Spoon
    into 6 nonstick 3-inch muffin tins, filling them.

3   Bake until a toothpick comes out clean and tops are tipped golden brown, 8
    to 10 minutes. Serve warm.

MAKES 6 MUFFINS

SIMPLE TIP *Muffin batter should be mixed with a few quick strokes, just enough to combine the ingredients. It should be slightly lumpy with a little flour still visible here and there.*

Rustic Onion Rolls

These rolls are crusted with golden onions, and chewy to eat. They have bumpy, roller-coaster tops and look like they were formed without too steady a hand. I think that's fun. Look for the dough in the refrigerated dairy case if your store carries it fresh. If not, try the frozen pizza section.

1 large egg
3 tablespoons dehydrated chopped onion
Flour
1 pound pizza dough

1   Preheat oven to 400°F. Lightly beat egg with 1 tablespoon water in a small bowl. Combine onion flakes with 3 tablespoons of the egg in a small bowl.

2   Flour a rolling surface and cut dough in half. Roll half into a rectangle roughly 4 x 8 inches. Spread with half of onion-egg mixture. Cut into quarters and transfer to a lightly floured cookie sheet. Repeat with other half.

3   Bake until rolls are risen and golden, about 15 minutes. Serve warm.

MAKES 8 ROLLS

SIMPLE TIP *Stop if the dough balks when you try to roll it. Instead, hold down one end of the dough and stretch it lengthwise with the other hand.*

DRESS IT UP *To make 8 rolls that look like snails, do this: Spread one rectangle with one-third of the onion-egg. Then loosely roll from the short end to form a cylinder. Repeat with the other piece of dough. Cut each cylinder into 4 pieces on the diagonal and spread the remaining onion-egg over their tops.*

VARIATION *Sprinkle the dough with sesame or poppy seeds. Or, turn it into "everything" rolls with both the seeds and the onion.*

Sesame Pitas

Everyone likes pita breads, especially when they're warm and slightly crisp. These go one step farther. They're brushed with olive oil and sprinkled with a Middle Eastern mix of sesame seeds and thyme before toasting.

4 pita breads, 6 inches in diameter
1 tablespoon extra-virgin olive oil
1 tablespoon sesame seeds
1 teaspoon dried thyme

1   Preheat oven to 400°F. Cut pitas in half.

2   Brush tops of breads with olive oil. Sprinkle with sesame seeds and then with thyme and salt to taste.

3   Lay breads on a cookie sheet. Bake 5 to 7 minutes, or until tops are golden and crisped. Serve hot.

4 SERVINGS

SIMPLE TIP *A toaster-oven works well, too, and faster than a conventional oven. The breads will be done in 2 or 3 minutes. The only downside is that they won't all fit at the same time.*

VARIATION *Sprinkle the pita breads with ground cumin to add an Indian touch.*

Garden Mashed Potatoes

When you boil potatoes in vegetable broth, they drink in the savory liquid and take on delicate vegetable flavor. How nice that you don't have to cut even a single carrot or stalk of celery!

1 1/2 pounds Yukon Gold or other boiling potatoes, peeled
2 1/2 cups vegetable broth
4 tablespoons butter, softened
3/4 teaspoon dried oregano

1 Cut potatoes into 1- to 1 1/2-inch pieces. Bring potatoes and broth to a boil in a large saucepan over high heat. Cover, lower heat to medium, and cook until potatoes are tender but not falling apart, 15 to 20 minutes.

2 Drain potatoes in a colander set inside a larger bowl. Reserve broth.

3 Return potatoes to pot over low heat. Mash, gradually adding butter and about ²/₃ cup broth. Season with salt and freshly ground pepper. Serve sprinkled with oregano

4 TO 5 SERVINGS

SIMPLE TIP *Vegetable broths vary a lot. Some are full of flavor and others are bland or even muddy tasting. Also, some are much saltier than others. I use the College Inn brand, which has a clean, light taste.*

Smashed Potatoes with Fresh Basil

Are you hankering for mashed potatoes but don't feel like peeling the spuds? Then have *smashed* potatoes. They offer all the pleasure with less of the work. When you cook the potatoes until just tender, they turn creamy when smashed. And they keep some big, satisfying lumps. My friend Marie makes hers with fruity olive oil and a handful of fresh basil at the end. This is how they're done.

1 1/2 pounds Yukon Gold potatoes
1/4 cup plus 2 tablespoons extra-virgin olive oil
1/2 cup fresh basil, torn into small pieces

1   Scrub potatoes and cut into 2-inch pieces.

2   In a large pot of lightly salted boiling water, cook potatoes until just tender, 15 to 20 minutes. Reserve 1/4 cup cooking water, then drain. Return potatoes to pot over low heat.

3 Gradually add olive oil and 2 tablespoons cooking water, stirring and chopping with side of a large spoon. Season with salt and pepper. Stir in additional water if potatoes seem dry. Stir in basil and serve hot.

4 TO 6 SERVINGS

VARIATION *Thinly slice the white and green parts of 2 scallions. Set the green part of 1 scallion aside. Heat 1 tablespoon butter in a medium saucepan over medium heat. Add the remaining 1 1/2 scallions, and cook until they wilt, about 2 minutes. Scrape into the mashed potatoes. Top each serving with a sprinkle of the reserved scallion top.*

Roasted Baked Potatoes

Just what are these guys, you say? Well, they've got brown, crunchy outsides and fluffy baked potato insides and are a cinch to make. You cut a couple of baking potatoes into long quarters and toss them with olive oil and cumin. Which ups their taste without screaming "spice." A hot oven does the rest.

2 Idaho potatoes
$1/4$ cup olive oil
1 tablespoon ground cumin

1   Preheat oven to 425°F. Scrub and dry potatoes. Quarter lengthwise.

2   Toss in a bowl with olive oil, cumin, $3/4$ teaspoon salt, and $1/4$ teaspoon freshly ground pepper. Lay cut side down on a baking pan. Scrape out remaining oil from bowl with a rubber spatula and drizzle on top.

3   Bake until potatoes are crusty, brown, and tender, about 30 minutes. Drizzle with oil in pan and serve hot.

4 SERVINGS

SIMPLE TIP *The potatoes brown best if roasted with a good inch of space around each piece. When they're done, slide a metal spatula underneath to loosen and lift if any have stuck to the pan.*

Sweet Potatoes with Creamy Orange-Thyme Butter

Who can resist a baked sweet potato with its soft, satiny flesh and honeyed taste? Not me. And it really doesn't need a thing to improve it. But a spoonful of this fresh orange butter certainly couldn't hurt. These particular potatoes are cut in half the long way to cook more quickly. Then they're baked face down in the pan so the cut parts turn appetizingly brown.

1 medium orange
$\frac{1}{8}$ teaspoon dried thyme
3 tablespoons butter, softened
2 medium-large sweet potatoes

1   Preheat oven to 425°F. Grate orange zest. Mix zest with thyme and 2 tablespoons of butter in a small bowl until creamy. Season lightly with salt and freshly ground pepper.

2   Scrub and dry sweet potatoes. Cut lengthwise in half. Spread remaining 1 tablespoon plain butter over cut surfaces. Lay cut side down on a baking

sheet. Roast until bottoms are golden brown, about 20 minutes. Turn and bake until tender, 10 to 15 minutes more.

3 Serve hot, topped with orange-thyme butter.

4 SERVINGS

SIMPLE TIP *It goes without saying that you can bake the potatoes whole. And serve them cut open with the butter dropped in. Or scoop out the flesh and mash it with the butter. Either way, you should double the amount of orange-thyme butter for 4 potatoes.*

DRESS IT UP *Fresh thyme is a wonderful thing. If you can get your hands on some, sprinkle fresh leaves over the butter-topped cooked potatoes (leaving out the dried thyme in the butter).*

Browned Onion Rice Pilaf

Rice pilaf is one of those great "serve-it-with-anything" side dishes. Its basic components are chopped onions, rice, and broth, and this one has those, too. Except here there's more onion and it's cooked until it turns really brown. That small touch gives the rice a deeper dimension.

2 tablespoons olive oil
1 large onion, thinly sliced
1 cup long-grain white rice
1 can (14 $1/2$ ounces) chicken broth

1   Heat olive oil in a large saucepan over medium-high heat. Cook onion, stirring occasionally, until well browned, about 5 minutes. Add rice and cook 30 seconds more, stirring.

2   Stir in broth plus $1/4$ cup water. Season with $1/2$ teaspoon salt. Bring to a boil, stirring. Then reduce heat to low so it simmers. Cover and cook 18 minutes.

3   Fluff rice grains with a fork. Serve hot, with a grinding of pepper over each serving.

4 TO 6 SERVINGS

VARIATION *Looking for a little pizzazz with your rice pilaf? Then scatter chopped Greek olives on top before serving.*

Savory Noodle Pie

This homey side dish is part Italian frittata and part crustless quiche. All together, it's a firm, pleasantly chewy custard of noodles, milk, eggs, and cheese, particularly good with grilled chops and chicken, or almost any kind of roast.

2 cups wide dried egg noodles

1 teaspoon softened butter

2 eggs

2 teaspoons Dijon mustard

1 cup milk

1 cup shredded Jarlsberg or Swiss cheese

1 Preheat oven to 350°F. Cook noodles in large saucepan of salted boiling water until pliable but still very firm, about 4 minutes. Drain and run under cold water; drain well.

2 Butter a shallow 9-inch baking dish. In a large bowl, lightly beat eggs with mustard. Gradually whisk in milk. Season with $1/2$ teaspoon salt and $1/8$ teaspoon freshly ground pepper. Stir in $3/4$ cup cheese.

3 Pour into dish and spread evenly. Sprinkle remaining cheese on top. Bake until edges puff slightly and a knife inserted in the center comes out clean, about 30 minutes. Cut into wedges and serve hot.

4 TO 6 SERVINGS

SIMPLE TIP *Bake the pie in an oven-to-table dish or cast-iron pan and cut it at the table.*

VARIATION *Mix in $1/4$ cup leftover, cooked vegetables such as small broccoli florets or chopped red bell pepper.*

Tomato Couscous

This rich-tasting couscous turns out all pumpkin colored from the tomatoes. And it is ever-so-slightly sweetened from a big pinch of cloves.

1 tablespoon butter
$1/2$ cup canned crushed tomatoes
$1/4$ teaspoon ground cloves
$3/4$ cup couscous

1   Melt butter in a medium saucepan over medium heat. Stir in tomatoes and cloves. Cook, stirring occasionally, until most of liquid cooks away, about 2 minutes.

2   Add $3/4$ cup water and $1/2$ teaspoon salt. Bring to a boil. Stir in the couscous, cover, and remove from the heat. Let sit 5 minutes.

3   Fluff grains with a fork and serve hot.

4 SERVINGS

VARIATION *Use olive oil instead of the butter.*

Salads
of All Sorts

Avocado Vinaigrette with Mustard and Lemon

This easygoing salad seems made for a balmy summer's night. But have it, naturally, whenever the fancy strikes. The dressing is a simple combination of puckery lemon juice and mustard balanced by sweet vinegar and olive oil. A spoonful or two enhances the creamy avocado to a "T."

1 tablespoon fresh lemon juice
2 teaspoons balsamic vinegar
2 teaspoons French Pommery coarse-grained mustard
$\frac{1}{4}$ cup extra-virgin olive oil
2 ripe avocados

1　Whisk together lemon juice, balsamic vinegar, and mustard in a small bowl. Gradually whisk in olive oil. Season with salt and freshly ground pepper.

2　Cut avocados in half lengthwise. Discard pits. Cut each piece lengthwise in half again, then peel off skins, which will come off easily.

3 Lay 2 avocado quarters on their sides on each plate. Dress with vinaigrette and serve.

4 SERVINGS

SIMPLE TIP *Substitute Dijon mustard for Pommery but use a little less because it's sharper.*

DRESS IT UP *Turn the avocados into a light summer meal by adding grilled sea scallops or shrimp. Sprinkle everything with chopped fresh herbs, such as chives, oregano, or tarragon.*

VARIATION *Sprinkle the dressed avocados with capers. Or set them on a lettuce leaf or two before dressing them.*

Balsamic Caesar Salad

Lust for Caesar salad? You bet. The combination of crisp leaves of romaine tossed in lemony garlic dressing and Parmesan cheese is unbeatable. And, in fact, the crisper the leaves, the better. This version incorporates all the garlic and cheese of the classic but adds yogurt for thickness and tang. Then it's lightly sweetened with balsamic vinegar. The result is a potent dressing just right for meaty romaine.

2 heads romaine lettuce
2 tablespoons balsamic vinegar
2 large garlic cloves, minced
$^1/_4$ cup plus 2 tablespoons extra-virgin olive oil
$^1/_4$ cup plain yogurt
3 tablespoons freshly grated Parmesan cheese

1 Pull off dark outer leaves of lettuce to reach crisp, lighter-colored ones. Tear or cut enough of these into pieces to measure 9 lightly packed cups. Wash and dry well.

2   Whisk balsamic vinegar and garlic together in a medium bowl. Gradually whisk in olive oil, then yogurt. Season with salt and freshly ground pepper.

3   Place lettuce in a large bowl and toss with dressing to lightly coat. Sprinkle with cheese and toss to coat. Serve right away.

4 TO 6 SERVINGS

SIMPLE TIP *Buy already washed hearts of romaine in a bag. All they need is tearing or cutting into pieces.*

DRESS IT UP *Olive oil–baked croutons are a natural addition. So are sliced radishes. For a luncheon or light supper salad, top with sliced grilled chicken or small fillets of grilled salmon.*

Carrot and Apple Salad with Tahini Dressing

The carrots, apples, and dates in this crunchy chopped salad are all naturally sweet, which makes them a harmonious lot. Their sweetness is balanced by the rich nuttiness of tahini, which is sesame seed paste, and brightened with lemon juice.

3 tablespoons tahini
3 tablespoons fresh lemon juice
2 medium carrots
1 small Granny Smith apple
6 pitted dates

1   Stir tahini and lemon juice together in a medium bowl. Stir in 2 to 2 1/2 tablespoons water to make a thick dressing that flows slightly. Season with salt and pepper.

2   Peel carrots. Core apple. Chop both into small pieces. Cut dates into small pieces.

3   Add carrots, apple, and dates to bowl; drizzle dressing on top and toss.

4 SERVINGS

SIMPLE TIP *The lemon juice thickens the tahini when it's mixed in. But it also makes it look strange. Don't worry, once the water is added, the dressing turns creamy again.*

DRESS IT UP *Serve the salad on pretty red-tipped lettuce leaves and sprinkle with toasted, chopped walnuts or pecans.*

VARIATION *Replace the dates with 1$\frac{1}{2}$ tablespoons raisins.*

Smoked Chicken and Mango Salad

This salad belongs on the list of essential summer-night suppers. What it is are smoky chunks of chicken tossed with sweet, lush mango in a tart lime and yogurt dressing. It's easily expanded, too, if you want. Simply serve on a bed of lovely lettuce leaves and garnish with radishes, cherry tomatoes, and sliced avocado. All you need to add is a crisp baguette.

6 tablespoons fresh lime juice

$^3/_4$ cup plain yogurt

1$^1/_2$ teaspoons ground cumin

1 ripe mango

1$^1/_2$ pounds smoked chicken or turkey breast

$^1/_4$ cup alfalfa sprouts

1 Place lime juice in a large bowl. Whisk in yogurt until smooth. Stir in cumin. Season with salt and freshly ground pepper.

2 Peel mango. Cut into $^3/_4$-inch cubes. Peel off and discard chicken skin. Cut into $^3/_4$-inch cubes. Add mango and smoked chicken to dressing and toss gently to coat.

3 Scatter sprouts over top and serve.

4 MAIN-COURSE SERVINGS

SIMPLE TIP *To prepare a mango, first cut a thin slice off the top and bottom. Stand it on end. Slice down just behind the skin to remove it in sections. Cut off the flesh in one piece from each wide side, cutting as closely as possible to the pit. Then slice down the edges to get one strip each. Now you can dice or slice the fruit any way you like.*

DRESS IT UP *Turn the salad into an elegant first course for 8. Thinly slice the smoked chicken and mango pieces lengthwise. Lay them on plates, alternating and overlapping slightly. Drizzle with dressing and scatter a few sprouts over top. Finally, place a perfect radish on top to pick up and eat out of hand.*

VARIATION *Substitute papaya or a firm-ripe melon for the mango.*

Warm Winter Chicken Salad with Lemon-Roquefort Dressing

The skinny strips of chicken that go into this salad simmer in a lemony dressing over the lowest possible heat, which seasons the strips and helps keep them moist. Then cheese is added and it is all tossed with the greens. All you need to add is crusty bread or toasted and buttered English muffins for sopping up the juices.

8 ounces mixed baby greens (mesclun)
$^2/_3$ cup slivered fennel bulb
$^1/_4$ cup fresh lemon juice
$^1/_2$ cup extra-virgin olive oil
1 pound skinless, boneless chicken breasts
$^1/_4$ cup crumbled Roquefort or other blue cheese

1   Place greens in a large salad bowl. Scatter fennel over top. Place lemon juice in a small bowl and gradually whisk in olive oil. Season with salt and freshly ground pepper.

2　Cut chicken crosswise into very thin strips. Heat dressing in a large skillet over low heat. Add strips and cook, stirring, until not completely white throughout, 2 to 3 minutes. (They will continue cooking as they cool.) Remove from heat. Stir in cheese and mash with back of a spoon.

3　Let cool until almost room temperature. Pour over greens and toss. Serve right away.

4　SERVINGS

SIMPLE TIP *To cut a fennel bulb, first cut it in half from top to bottom. Cut out the cores. Peel off the layers, then cut each into thin strips parallel with the grain. It's best to use the inner layers for eating raw because they're more tender.*

DRESS IT UP *Stir a handful of pine nuts or chopped walnuts into the pan about a minute before the chicken is done.*

VARIATION *Use a firm, tangy goat cheese instead of the Roquefort.*

Lemon Coleslaw

I admit to having a soft spot for coleslaw. And I prefer ones in fairly traditional style, meaning, the cabbage should be shredded as finely as possible and be dressed in a creamy sauce with a touch of sharpness. This one fits the bill, then raises the ante with its terrific, tart lemon taste. The recipe calls for cutting the cabbage, but already shredded "classic coleslaw" mix works, too. Use half of a bag for the recipe, or go ahead and use the whole thing. Just double the sauce.

1 small head green cabbage
1 large lemon
$1/2$ teaspoon powdered mustard
$1/3$ cup mayonnaise
$1/2$ teaspoon sugar

1   Cut cabbage in half from top to bottom. Cut out and discard core. Finely shred enough to measure 4 cups.

2   Grate lemon zest. Squeeze 1 tablespoon of the juice. Place mustard in a large bowl and stir in juice. Stir in mayonnaise until smooth. Stir in lemon zest and sugar. Season with salt and freshly ground pepper.

3   Add cabbage and combine well. Let coleslaw sit until its juices flow, 3 to 5 minutes, then serve.

3 TO 4 SERVINGS

DRESS IT UP *Serve the coleslaw in a pretty bowl. Ring the top with cherry or grape tomatoes alternated with slices or wedges of hard-cooked egg. And maybe some big, fat purple Greek olives.*

Sautéed Corn and Red Pepper Salad

My friend Marie swears by frozen white corn. She says, "With it around, it's so easy to toss something together when I get home from work in a comatose state!" One of her favorite ways is a salad with sweet peppers and black olives. Inspired by her, I imagined the corn and red peppers sautéed in garlic olive oil for just a minute so they stay crunchy, then splashed with vinegar to become a salad. It's good at any temperature: hot, warm, tepid, or chilled.

1 medium red bell pepper
2 large garlic cloves
1 1/2 tablespoons olive oil
2 cups frozen white shoepeg corn
1 1/2 tablespoons cider vinegar
1 tablespoon finely diced red onion

1   Cut bell pepper into small dice. Lightly crush garlic with side of a knife.

2   Heat olive oil in a large skillet over low heat. Cook garlic, turning once, until golden on both sides, about 3 minutes. Discard garlic.

3   Stir sweet pepper into oil. Immediately add corn. Heat, stirring occasionally, until it defrosts, about 2 minutes. Stir in vinegar, then remove from heat. Season with salt and freshly ground pepper. Serve with red onion sprinkled on top.

4 SERVINGS

DRESS IT UP *Sprinkle fresh chives with the red onion over the salad when it's served. Or, if you're serving it room temperature or chilled, toss in a handful of torn fresh basil leaves at the last minute.*

VARIATION *Marie tells me that when she has more than an "eighth of an ounce of energy," she sautés some shrimp and then piles the whole thing on top of a toasted pita.*

Red Lettuce with Red Fruit in Cream Dressing

Don't be scared off by the cream. It dresses this elegant salad in the most delicate possible fashion. And when you look to see what the red fruit is going to be, you might be thinking, "Oh, yeah, tomatoes but not sure about those plums." Well, their sweetness plays off the tarter tomatoes and light lemony dressing in a distinctly pleasing way.

1 head red-tipped leaf lettuce
12 grape or cherry tomatoes
2 medium purple plums
$1\frac{1}{2}$ tablespoons fresh lemon juice
$\frac{1}{3}$ cup heavy cream

1 Tear enough lettuce into pieces to measure 6 lightly packed cups. Wash and dry it well. Cut the tomatoes into halves. Cut plums into thin wedges.

2 Place lemon juice in a medium bowl and gradually whisk in cream. Continue whisking until cream thickens slightly. Season lightly with salt and freshly ground pepper.

3 Place lettuce in a large salad bowl. Spoon over dressing, then toss to coat lightly. Divide among plates. Arrange tomatoes and plums over salads and serve right away.

4 SERVINGS

VARIATIONS *Garnish the salad with sliced or diced avocado. Or use the dressing alone over any sort of sweet, fresh fruit or a mixture.*

Grilled Shrimp Salad with Feta Cheese and Olives

These shrimp can be a light dinner for four or a first course for eight. But whichever you choose, count on whole, lightly charred shrimp under a jumble of lusty black olives and crumbled feta with oregano. And if dinner is how you go, serve good chewy bread with olive oil for dipping, followed by some sinful dessert.

24 kalamata or other ripe Greek olives
1/4 cup plus 2 tablespoons extra-virgin olive oil
2 tablespoons fresh lemon juice
1/2 cup crumbled feta cheese
1/2 teaspoon dried oregano
1 1/2 pounds large shrimp, peeled and deveined

1   Prepare a hot fire in a barbecue grill. Pit and chop olives. In a medium bowl, whisk 1/4 cup plus 2 teaspoons olive oil with lemon juice. Stir in feta, olives, and oregano. Season generously with freshly ground pepper.

2   Dry shrimp on paper towels. Toss in a bowl with remaining 4 teaspoons oil. Thread onto skewers.

3 Grill, turning once, until cooked through with edges lightly charred, about 4 minutes. Slide shrimp off skewers and arrange on plates. Stir dressing, spoon over shrimp, and serve.

4 MAIN-COURSE SERVINGS

SIMPLE TIP *While pitted kalamata olives are commonly sold, pitting olives yourself is easy. Press down on one or two at a time with the side of a large knife. When they split open slightly, you can pull out the pits.*

DRESS IT UP *Lay the shrimp over slices of bread brushed with olive oil and grilled or over slices of beautiful ripe tomatoes. Either way, dress them with the feta and olives and sprinkle with fresh oregano, instead of using dried.*

VARIATION *Chop the cooked shrimp and toss them with the dressing for a completely chopped salad. Add some pasta, too, if you want, and more olive oil, if it needs it. When the weather doesn't cooperate, the shrimp can be sautéed or even boiled instead of grilled.*

Baby Spinach Salad with Warm Bacon Dressing

Buying a bag of baby spinach already washed and ready to go
makes salad that much easier. Here's a variation on the classic
spinach and bacon duo that skips the traditional mushrooms.
This one has crunchy red onion and fresh lemon juice, which
balance the taste of the smoky meat and earthy greens.

4 strips bacon
$1/2$ small red onion
$1^1/2$ teaspoons Dijon mustard
1 tablespoon fresh lemon juice
$2^1/2$ tablespoons extra-virgin olive oil, plus more if needed
1 bag (6 ounces) baby spinach

1   Cook bacon in a skillet over low heat until crisp, 6 to 8 minutes. Drain on
    paper towels. Reserve 2 tablespoons of fat. Reserve skillet. Thinly slice onion.

2   Place mustard in a small bowl and whisk in lemon juice. Whisk in bacon fat
    followed by olive oil. Make up the difference with more oil if less than 2
    tablespoons fat. Season lightly with salt and freshly ground pepper.

3 Place spinach in a large salad bowl. Add red onion slices. Crumble bacon over top. Warm dressing in skillet over low heat, 30 to 60 seconds. Pour over salad, toss, and serve.

4 TO 6 SERVINGS

VARIATION *When you toss in a handful of diced Swiss cheese and toasted walnuts, this salad can make a good, light supper for two. Serve with Sesame Pitas (page 154) or thick slices of whole-grain bread.*

Watercress Salad with Pears and Creamy Goat Cheese Dressing

This salad is a happy blend of tastes and textures. It has a smooth, mildly tangy dressing, which lightly coats the peppery watercress. And there's sweet, juicy pear to provide gentle contrast for it all.

$1/4$ cup plus 2 tablespoons log-style goat cheese, 3 ounces
$1/4$ cup milk
2 tablespoons extra-virgin olive oil
$1^{1}/_{2}$ tablespoons fresh lemon juice
1 bunch watercress
1 ripe pear

1   Puree $1/4$ cup goat cheese, milk, olive oil, and lemon juice in a blender until smooth, about 1 minute. Season with salt and freshly ground pepper. Set dressing aside.

2   Trim lower third of stems from watercress. Cut pear in half, core, and thinly slice lengthwise. Arrange slices fanned out on plates.

3   Toss watercress with $\frac{1}{4}$ cup of dressing to lightly coat. Mound next to pears. Drizzle remaining dressing over salads. Crumble remaining cheese over tops. Finish with a grinding of pepper and serve.

4 SERVINGS

DRESS IT UP *Toasted, chopped walnuts are a perfect, crunchy addition to the salad. Scatter them over the top of each serving.*

Simple Sweets

Roasted Fresh Apricots with Crème Fraîche

I don't know if this is true for you, but too often the apricots I've had are sadly disappointing. Here's a recipe, then, that improves even mediocre fruit by roasting it. Surrounded by heat, the apricots pick up a jamlike intensity but don't lose their wonderful tart taste. They're delicious served warm in their buttery syrup and capped with cool cream.

1 pound fresh apricots
$1/4$ cup sugar
$1^1/2$ tablespoons unsalted butter
3 tablespoons crème fraîche

1 Preheat oven to 400°F. Cut apricots in half and remove pits.

2 Arrange apricots in a single layer in a baking pan. Sprinkle sugar over fruit and toss. Break butter into small pieces and scatter over apricots.

3 Bake until just beginning to collapse and pan juices are clear, 10 to 12 minutes. Serve warm, with crème fraîche on top.

4 SERVINGS

SIMPLE TIP *If any of the sugar in the pan hasn't dissolved when the apricots are done, add a little water to the pan. Then remove the apricots, set the pan over low heat, and stir until the juices turn clear.*

DRESS IT UP *Before spooning over the syrup, garnish each serving with fresh raspberries or blackberries. Then top with crème fraîche.*

VARIATION *Use quartered large peaches or plums cut in half instead of the apricots. Sour cream can replace the crème fraîche.*

Cinnamon Sugar Bananas

Cooked bananas have the sweetest, deepest, most intense banana taste. These particular ones are rolled in butter, then sprinkled with cinnamon sugar and baked.

3$\frac{1}{2}$ teaspoons sugar

$\frac{1}{4}$ teaspoon ground cinnamon

4 ripe bananas without spots

2 tablespoons unsalted butter, melted

1 Preheat oven to 375°F. Mix sugar and cinnamon in a small bowl. Peel, then cut bananas on the diagonal into quarters.

2 Lay in a single layer in a baking pan, leaving space between pieces. Pour melted butter over bananas and roll to coat. Sprinkle cinnamon sugar over all sides without rolling.

3 Bake without turning until tender but intact, about 10 minutes. Serve hot or warm.

4 SERVINGS

SIMPLE TIP *If you roll the bananas in the sugar, it sticks to the pan instead of the bananas.*

DRESS IT UP *Sprinkle the cooked bananas with grated or finely chopped dark chocolate. Top them with whipped cream, too, if you want. Or make ice cream sundaes with the chocolate-sprinkled bananas and whipped cream.*

Chocolate Cupcakes

If you're like me, chocolate cake is one of life's little necessities. Happily, here are 6 moist, deep chocolatey cupcakes with shiny glazed tops for when the need strikes. Nice, too, that the batter can be stirred together in one bowl. And to do that, I use a large rubber spatula because it easily smooths out any lumps, then scrapes out the last bit of batter in the bowl into the baking cups. For large cupcakes, fill five muffin cups three-quarters of the way instead of making six.

$3/4$ cup plus 3 tablespoons sugar

$1/3$ cup plus 2 tablespoons unsweetened cocoa powder

$1/2$ teaspoon baking soda

3 tablespoons unsalted butter, cut into small pieces

$1/4$ cup sour cream

$3/4$ cup all-purpose flour

1 egg

1   Preheat oven to 350°F with a rack in the center. Place $3/4$ cup sugar, $1/3$ cup cocoa, the baking soda, $1/8$ teaspoon salt, and butter in a large bowl. Bring a generous $1/3$ cup water to a boil. Measure $1/3$ cup and pour over ingredients.

2 Stir until butter melts and batter is smooth, about 1 minute. Stir in 3 tablespoons of sour cream until smooth. Stir in flour and then egg until smooth. Spoon batter into 6 paper-lined 3-inch muffin cups, filling by about half. Bake until a few moist crumbs cling to a toothpick, 25 to 28 minutes.

3 Bring remaining 3 tablespoons sugar with 2 tablespoons water to a boil in a small saucepan over medium heat, stirring. Cook until clear, about 30 seconds. Remove from heat and whisk in remaining cocoa until smooth. Whisk in remaining 1 tablespoon sour cream until smooth. Spoon glaze over tops of cakes.

MAKES 6 CUPCAKES

SIMPLE TIP *To measure flour accurately, first stir it slightly in the container. Spoon it to overflowing into a nesting type measuring cup without shaking or settling the flour. Then sweep across the top of the cup with a chopstick or back of a knife.*

VARIATION *Instead of the glaze, blanket the tops with confectioners' sugar while the cupcakes are still hot. Use $1/2$ teaspoon sugar for each and press it through a small strainer held above the cakes. And call them Powdered Sugar Cupcakes.*

Chocolate Mocha Sundae

Chocolate and coffee is a win-win flavor combination. Not least when they come together as a sauce for ice cream. This recipe makes enough sauce for one or two scoops all around. So if you want killer-size sundaes, double the recipe.

2 1/2 ounces semisweet chocolate, chopped
2 1/2 teaspoons instant coffee granules
1/4 cup plus 2 tablespoons heavy cream
2 tablespoons superfine sugar
Vanilla, chocolate, or coffee ice cream

1   Put chopped chocolate in a medium bowl. Sprinkle with coffee granules.

2   Place cream and sugar in a small saucepan over low heat. Stir to dissolve sugar, 30 to 60 seconds. Increase heat to medium and bring to a boil. Immediately pour hot syrup over chocolate and coffee.

3   Let sit about 30 seconds, then whisk slowly until smooth. Scoop ice cream into bowls and spoon sauce on top.

4 SERVINGS

SIMPLE TIPS *Chop the chocolate into small pieces to make sure the cream melts it.*

The sauce can be served warm, at room temperature, or chilled.

DRESS IT UP *It goes without saying that whipped cream is a great addition. But so are two vanilla cream wafers stuck into each sundae. Or a sprinkle of salted peanuts, or the Buttery Glazed Pecans on page 214.*

White Chocolate Mousse with Oreos

To make this creamy dessert, follow these pointers for a luscious result:

- be sure the water is not more than hot while the chocolate is melting;
- remove the chocolate from the water bath as soon as it melts; and
- let the chocolate cool a bit before combining it with the whipped cream.

"Okay," you say, "but where do the Oreos come in?" Easy, they stick out of the snowy white mousse as dark chocolate scoops for eating.

6 ounces white chocolate

$^3/_4$ cup heavy cream

4 chocolate cream–filled Oreo cookies

1 Break chocolate into pieces. Melt in a double boiler over hot water, stirring, about 3 minutes. Remove and let cool until barely warm, 3 to 4 minutes.

2 Whip cream just until it mounds softly. Stir about one-fourth into chocolate. Fold chocolate cream into remaining whipped cream until combined. Divide among bowls and refrigerate 30 to 60 minutes, until set.

3 Twist cookies to separate halves. Stick 2 halves part way into each serving and serve.

4 SERVINGS

DRESS IT UP *For an elegant finish, serve the mousse in stemmed glasses and sprinkle with chopped bittersweet chocolate instead of the cookies.*

Fresh Peach Cake

Juicy peaches and delicately sweet flavor make this cake an innocent charmer. It is lightly crisp on the outside and moist on the inside. You make it in just one bowl with one sliced peach and serve it warm. If you like, garnish each serving with more sliced peaches and whipped cream alongside.

1^1/$_2$ tablespoons unsalted butter

1 large ripe peach

2 large eggs

^{1}/$_3$ cup plus 1 tablespoon sugar

^{1}/$_2$ cup milk

^{3}/$_4$ cup all-purpose flour

2 teaspoons baking powder

1 Preheat oven to 425°F with a rack in the center. Butter an 8-inch round glass or ceramic baking dish with ^{1}/$_2$ tablespoon of butter. Cut peach in half and discard pit. Thinly slice peach and arrange half over bottom of dish.

2 In a large bowl, whisk together eggs and ^{1}/$_3$ cup sugar. Whisk in milk. Stir in flour, baking powder, and a pinch of salt until smooth. Pour batter over peach

slices. Arrange remaining slices on top like spokes of a wheel. Sprinkle 1 table-spoon sugar over top and dot with remaining 1 tablespoon butter.

3 Bake until top is golden and a toothpick comes out clean, 23 to 25 minutes. Serve warm, cut into wedges.

6 SERVINGS

DRESS IT UP *Serve a small pitcher of heavy cream so everyone can pour some over his or her piece.*

VARIATION *Sprinkle the top with grated nutmeg before sugaring and baking. Use a pear instead of the peach.*

Honey-Baked Pears

These pears are cut in half, sweetened, then baked to tenderness in their skin. Their honeyed juices mingle with butter and nutmeg in the pan and caramelize to a golden hue.

2 firm, ripe Bartlett or Anjou pears
1 tablespoon butter, cut into 4 pieces
$1^1\!/_2$ tablespoons honey
$^1\!/_2$ teaspoon grated nutmeg

1   Preheat oven to 375°F. Cut pears lengthwise in half. Core with a melon baller. Cut a sliver off each bottom so they lie, cavity up, without rocking.

2   Place pear halves in an 8-inch square baking pan. Place 1 piece of butter in each cavity. Drizzle honey over pieces, then sprinkle with nutmeg.

3   Bake until pears are tender and pan juices are lightly thickened and golden, 25 to 30 minutes. Serve warm with pan juices spooned over pears.

4 SERVINGS

SIMPLE TIP *If a wooden skewer easily penetrates the pears, they're ready. If the juices aren't caramelized, first pour the juices from the pear cavities into the pan. Then transfer the pears to plates and bake the juices in the pan for a few more minutes.*

DRESS IT UP *For a delicious addition, drop a teaspoonful or so of cool sour cream onto each pear when they're served.*

Pecan Candy

Warning: These candies can become addictive! They are easy to make and their sweet chewiness and crunch makes them even easier to eat.

4 tablespoons unsalted butter
1 cup pecan pieces
$^1/_4$ cup honey

1   Melt butter in a medium skillet over low heat. Stir in the pecans and honey.

2   Cook, stirring occasionally, until honey turns golden brown, about 3 minutes.

3   Immediately pour onto a plate and spread with the back of a spoon (do not touch; it can burn). Let cool until warm, 6 to 8 minutes. Press into 16 roughly shaped balls.

MAKES 16 CANDIES

SIMPLE TIP *Coat the spoon with vegetable oil before measuring the honey, and it will slide right out.*

DRESS IT UP *Dip half of each candy into melted semisweet chocolate. Eat as is or serve them with long-stemmed strawberries when they're in season.*

Raspberries with Butterscotch Cream

Simply cooking together butter, brown sugar, and cream produces a sauce that shows off plump, fresh raspberries to their utmost. Particularly if the berries are at room temperature, when their flavor is best.

$1/2$ cup heavy cream
$1/4$ cup packed light brown sugar
$1^1/2$ tablespoons unsalted butter
2 containers (6 ounces each) fresh raspberries

1 Bring cream, brown sugar, and butter to a boil in a medium saucepan over medium heat. Boil, stirring occasionally, until reduced to $2/3$ cup, about 3 minutes. Remove from heat and let cool.

2 Divide raspberries among bowls and spoon sauce over berries.

4 SERVINGS

DRESS IT UP *Scatter pieces of chopped dark chocolate over the sauced berries.*

Blueberries with Maple-Orange Yogurt Sauce

Tangy yogurt brings out the sweet side of blueberries. Particularly when maple syrup and fresh orange zest get into the act.

1^1/$_2$ pints blueberries
1 cup plain yogurt
4 teaspoons maple syrup
2 teaspoons vanilla extract
Grated zest of 1 orange

1 Pick through berries to remove stems. Rinse and drain well.

2 Mix yogurt, maple syrup, vanilla, and orange zest in a small bowl.

3 Divide blueberries among bowls. Spoon sauce over berries and serve.

4 SERVINGS

VARIATION *The sauce is also good over fresh raspberries and blackberries or a combo of berries and melon.*

Strawberries with Brown Sugar Sauce

This dessert is little more than strawberries glossed with a simple syrup of orange juice and brown sugar. The "little more," though, is what makes it more than a little special. The syrup is poured over while still warm, which brings out the sweet juiciness of the berries.

1 quart strawberries
$^1/_2$ cup orange juice
$^1/_4$ cup packed light brown sugar
2 tablespoons unsalted butter

1 Rinse and hull strawberries. Dry on paper towels. Cut in half or quarter if large.

2 Bring orange juice, brown sugar, and butter to a boil in a small saucepan over medium heat. Boil, stirring occasionally, until reduced to $^1/_2$ cup syrupy liquid, about 5 minutes. Let cool to warm.

3 Place strawberries in bowls. Spoon sauce over berries and serve.

4 SERVINGS

SIMPLE TIP *Be sure the berries are at room temperature. Their flavor will be at its best.*

DRESS IT UP *Top the glossed berries with whipped cream or crème fraîche and sprinkle with toasted sliced almonds.*

VARIATION *Blueberries and blackberries are terrific with the sauce, too, or peeled and sliced fresh peaches.*

Buttery Glazed Pecan Sundae

Pecans turn crunchy and sweet when they're cooked in butter and sugar until caramelized. And when sprinkled over vanilla ice cream, they taste like butter pecan ice cream turned inside out. But you certainly don't have to stick to vanilla. Any kind of ice cream is just as good.

4 teaspoons unsalted butter
$^1/_2$ cup pecan pieces
$1^1/_2$ tablespoons sugar
Ice cream

1   Melt butter in a small skillet over low heat. Stir in pecans and sugar.

2   Cook, stirring occasionally, until sugar melts, then turns deep gold, 2 to 4 minutes. Immediately pour onto a plate and spread with a back of a spoon (do not touch; it can burn). Let cool, then break into individual nuts or small clusters.

3   Scoop ice cream into bowls and scatter pecans over top.

4 SERVINGS

SIMPLE TIP *A heavy skillet is best for melting and caramelizing the sugar. However, if the sugar isn't perfectly melted whatever pan you use, just call the nuts Sugared Pecans, in honor of the crystals that cling to them.*

DRESS IT UP *Spoon some Chocolate Mocha Sauce (page 200), over the ice cream and then follow with pecans. Whipped cream, too, would be great.*

Index